WHOSE CHURCH IS THIS ANYWAY?

*130 Sympathetic, Cavalier,
Outrageous and
Hilarious Letters
to the Parish Pastor*

ROBERT JOHN VERSTEEG

C.S.S. Publishing Company, Inc.
Lima, Ohio

WHOSE CHURCH IS THIS ANYWAY?

The quotation on page 63 is reprinted with permission from *The Uses of Enchantment: The Meaning and Importance of Fairy Tales,* by Bruno Bettelheim, Copyright Alfred A. Knopf, Inc., page 310.

The quotation on page 95 is reprinted with permission from *Dance: A Basic Educational Technique,* by Miriam Winslow, Copyright 1980 Dance Horizons, New York, page 81.

Drawings in this volume were created by the author.

Library of Congress Cataloging in Publication Data

Versteeg, Robert John, 1930-
    Whose church is this anyway?

    1. Clergy — Anecdotes, facetiae, satire, etc.
2. Imaginary letters. I. Title.
PN6231.C5V47 1985   816'.54   85-13282
ISBN 0-89536-767-X

5874 / ISBN 0-89536-767-X

For Donna

West Ohio Conference
471 E. Broad St. Suite P
Columbus, Ohio

My Dear Brother Versteeg,

No, I'm afraid I can't write a Preface or a recommendation for your book.

However, I want you to know that I do appreciate what you tried to do with these brief pieces — relax the reader with humor and then give the reader a lift for the day.

I also do appreciate that these are sparks struck from the anvil of parish life, and I know you think of the book as a kind of tribute to the wonderful people of the Point Place United Methodist Church you served in Toledo.

But on the other hand, I happen to know that you stole the whole idea from your brother, Rev. Virgil N. Versteeg, that distinguished servant of the Lord: making up funny letters from imaginary parishioners was his idea.

While I believe that nothing is so salutary in our spiritual walk as healthy humor, and although your friends and colleagues have encouraged you, frankly, I would have trouble recommending such a frivolous book as an addition to anyone's library. To the bathroom, maybe.

Yes, I do remember that twice in the past I have been instrumental in allowing you to minister — first as your seminary president and then as your bishop — but by now I have learned better than, with two strikes on me, to let myself be jammed by a ball high and inside.

However, I do wish you luck with your book. You need it.

Advisedly,

Bishop Bright Roader

FALL

FALLING FORWARD AND
STUDYING STATUES

666 Shoehorn Manor
Toledo, Ohio

1 September

Versteeg:

I'm not going to set foot inside that church nor contribute one red cent as long as you are the pastor there.

Nothing personal, understand. It's just a question of whose church this is.

I've heard about the abominations you are committing in the sanctuary — singing children's songs, teaching songs that are not in The Methodist Hymnal, baptizing at the door of the church, standing out in the open talking to people instead of preaching behind the pulpit where a preacher belongs, changing the announcements, changing the offering, changing the recessional, changing everything! What do you think you're trying to do?

Knock off with the folksy and keep things smooth, solemn, and dignified the way they were before you got here.

Whose church do you think this is, anyway — yours or mine?

Forthrightly,

Henrietta Peckingham

MANNY'S GYM
Four Seasons Drive
Toledo, Ohio

September 3

Hey, Rev,

Welcome to the team! I caught your first pitch Sunday.
I thought maybe you wouldn't mind some friendly coachin: if you wanna get through to some of the knothead leagues here, you gotta talk their langwidge.

Us guys like sports, so if you could kinda be like St Paul an talk some sports, you got a better chance of makin a hit an advancin the Kingdome.

Some of the guys didnt do to hot with them books they used in school, so they ain't all as literat as me. But the education we got in Sports is second to none. A book is somethin you look at; a sport is somethin you do — an that's why we learnt sports bettern books.

An like the Iron Duke said, "The war was won on eatin an the playin fields."

Way I see it, that's what we gotta do to make the Lord's team: get it outta the play book an onto the playin field — stop lookin an start doin.

You can count on me. I'll play ball with you from the openin whistle to the final gun.

Your pal,

Hulk Hagarson

7 Camelot Circle
Toledo, Ohio

September 5

Dear Pastor Bob,

I'm a push-over for the Romance of Trains.
Best of all I like the caboose.
My idea of a perfect home — especially a retirement home — would be a caboose.

For me, completion isn't signified by the final buzzer, the last whistle, or The Fat Lady Who Sings. For me closure is a caboose.

The caboose is the "fun thing" you look forward to (backward to?) at the end of the train. Engines, coal cars, freight cars, tank cars, flat cars — they all lead up to the fine finale of the caboose.

The caboose is the Snoopy of the railroad kingdom. It never takes itself too seriously, it never tries to deny its nature; it just jauntily revels in bringing up the rear with an absurd grace.

The caboose is always a kind of surprise happy ending — a sign of the triumph of hope-against-hope. The end is grace.

The caboose-like spirit is what Jesus had in mind when he promised that the last would be first and that the debonair would inherit the earth.

'Board!

Guinevere Jones

GUINEVERE JONES

ATTILA D. HUNN, D.D.S.
Canal Route #3
Toledo, Ohio

September 7

Dear Mr. Versteeg,

Let me explain your root canal.

I will remove the nerve from your tooth and fill its empty space.

Although the tooth will then, for all intents and purposes, be dead, it will remain in place and do its job just as if it were alive.

It will be just like a Christian who has lost his nerve.

No one will know the difference, except that you won't have any feeling in the tooth.

Unlike a soul, you see, a tooth does not need inner nourishment and has no need to keep growing.

Sincerely yours,

Attila D. Hunn, D.D.S.

P.S. May we please have something on your account?

Heart of the Forest
Black Mountain
North Carolina

September 8

Dear Bob,

These are my grasshopper days.

I know that as soon as I run through the forest the grasshoppers will begin to scatter — flying up in front of me.

I realize that in the city where you have gone to live "grasshoppers" have stings and are served in glasses, but I'm thinking of Aesop's story about the allegedly improvident grasshopper who fiddled through the summer while the industrious ant labored to hoard up food for the winter. I'm for the grasshopper.

Some of my friends, like you and other work-ethic ants, rue summer's lost opportunities; but me, I think fiddling's fine.

This past summer I have said "Yes" to every opportunity to gaze into a brook, to doze in a meadow, to dally with the daisies in the dell. I've inhaled to the bottom of my lungs every odor I've smelled, I've felt every rock I've touched, watched every bird I've seen, listened to every sound I've heard. I have sung every song that came into my mind, I have drunk every sunset; I have slept every night.

I have fiddled and feasted full of life enough to last the winter long.

Time comes, the writer of Ecclesiastes warns, when the grasshopper becomes a burden, and that time is when life becomes unbearable. Before it's too late, try a little grasshopping for yourself.

May your autumn be filled with grasshopper days!

Truly yours,

Jonathan Woodman

RABBIT RUN VOLKSWAGON INC.
13 Upshaft Drive
Toledo, Ohio

September 11

Pastor Vorshtag!

I am of course regretful to hear that, since you acquired it new seventeen months ago, your Volkswagen Rabbit has experienced nine breakdowns for a rate of better than one breakdown per every two months.

But what did you expect for $8,OOO?

As for your alternator burning out twice, each time after precisely 15,000 miles, you have to remember that with electrical equipment one never knows.

No, I regret we cannot replace only the rotor in the alternator, because the spare parts and the labor involved in replacing the rotor would cost you more than to replace the entire unit.

Maybe you can understand it better if you compare it to salvation:

In order to repair his personality, a person keeps trying to replace parts of himself, but he only keeps breaking down.

What he needs is a whole new person. "You must be born anew."

Same mit der alternator.

Your bill is $107.65.

'Wiedersehen!

Wolfgang von Krankcase
Service Manager

362636 Starlet Drive
Hollywood, California

September 13

Dear V.,

At choir practice tonight the director handed out a new anthem based on Psalm 119, the 33rd verse.

But the alto behind me was busy reading the musical notes and so she mis-read the words and with all her heart sang out:

"Teach me, O Lord, the way of thy *statues!*"

Now you know what's wrong: we've been studying the ways of statues.

All across the country there are churches filled with congregations studying to be the Lord's statues. They don't do anything; they just stand there pat, pure, or pigeoned.

The Lord's *statutes* — that is, his laws — are not for the immovable, but for flesh-and-blood people on the go.

And that's "on the go" *forward,* as in, "Brother, are you going on to perfection?" — not petrifaction.

I wonder if Lot's wife was an alto?

Luv a bunch!

Gloria Glitz

ATTILA D. HUNN, D.D.S.
Canal Route #3
Toledo, Ohio

September 15

Dear Mr. Versteeg,

Yes, it is all right to come back to have the crown we put on your tooth adjusted.

As I told you, your crown is on a dead tooth which — like a dead soul — has no feeling.

As with your tooth, if your conscience never twinges nor your spirit experiences discomfort, it may not necessarily be because you are perfect, but perhaps because you are spiritually dead.

At any rate, the adjustment will take only a few moments.

If people were as sensitive to their spiritual crowns as they are to their dental crowns, your pews would be as busy as my chairs.

Yours for more sensitive
crowns,

Attila D. Hunn, D.D.S.

P.S. May we please have something on your account?

666 Shoehorn Manor
Toledo, Ohio

18 September

Versteeg:

I still haven't met you, and judging by the asinine things I read in your church newsletter, I'm going to keep it that way.

So now you're going to teach married couples how to fight, are you? Isn't that just splendid!

Married couples, Versteeg, should not fight.

If a disagreement looms, one should walk away and refuse to become involved. That's always been my rule.

My husband, Caedman, and I never had one single fight in twenty-three years of wedded bliss — until the day he left me to marry my sister-in-law.

Now they fight all the time. Serves him right.

Not that I really care.

Whatever happened to "Blessed are the peacemakers"?

I'm sending a copy of this letter to our District Superintendent and Bishop, in hopes that they will remove you as rapidly as possible.

Do you think our District Superintendent or our Bishop ever fight with their wives? Such lovely couples!

Forthrightly,

Henrietta Peckingham

50 Hugenot Drive
Toledo, Ohio

September 19

Dear Reverend Versteeg,

I'm sorry I ran into you on Secor Road the other day.
You know how it was raining, and when you stopped for
that traffic light at Farmer Jack's, I put on my brakes, too, but
I knew right away there was no way I could stop in time, and I
could only watch while my car skidded and caught yours on the
tail end.

(There's a pun there: your car has a caught-on tail end.
Catch on? Caught-on tail — "cotton tail." Your Rabbit. Get
it? Everything has a lighter side.)

I'm glad your car didn't hurt the car in front of you when
the impact slammed you into it, and I hope the damage to your
front end isn't as extensive as it looked.

The policewoman gave me a citation for following too closely. It's made me think how we can get in trouble by following
too closely; and I thought you, being a minister and all, would
appreciate it.

I mean, following the crowd or following the wrong example. We think we can always stop when we want to, but then
things get out of control and *smash!* — caught on tail!

And not everything we run into in life has a shock-absorbing
bumper. A person can get hurt.

I hope your neck isn't sore anymore.
Again, I'm sorry it happened.

Sincerely yours,

Marie Saulterre

362636 Starlet Drive
Hollywood, California

September 21

Dear V.,

Sorry to hear about your car troubles. Cars can be a vexation.

You know the new one I just bought? First day in the grocery-store parking lot and guess what: yep — door dents.

But that's life — if you have nerve enough to leave the garage, you're gonna get a few dents.

I figure if you can keep the motor running and get where you're headed — and let's face it, most Americans do it with more comfort than most other people in this world — then the little door-dents of life, unpleasant as they may be, are not catastrophes.

But we sometimes have as much trouble keeping our perspective about the important things in life as we do about cars.

From the land of the Great White Freeways,

Luv a Bunch!

Gloria Glitz

Heart of the Forest
Black Mountain
North Carolina

September 23

Dear Bob,

When you left our life of play here in the woods and went back into the real world, I warned you not to take up the sword of satire again. Satire is too difficult a blade — even in Toledo — for you to manage.

Satire and subtlety don't mix. Satire is a broadsword; it requires a relentless slashing attack. When you try to be subtle with satire, you are trying to use it instead like a fencer's foil. Satire wants more a cutting edge than a puncturing point, because ignorance is chain mail.

You are too subtle by far (and you know which beast the Bible accuses of being subtle!).

Take the matter of these letters for your parish newsletter. Even if you were to state plainly that you and you alone are the culprit responsible for writing them — that you yourself write each one of them under such cloyingly obvious pen names — there are folks who are still going to be confused. You are too subtle by far.

I know how devious you are, too. You'll begin to tell me that there are many ways to communicate Christ, and that the Word may sometimes be spoken more effectively in satire than in broadsides. That's all very well. But as you know, I am for simplicity and straightforwardness. I think you'll find that the great communicators of the Word have spoken it lovingly and simply.

Don't forget — there in the city — our simple life here in the woods; because no matter how complicated you make it there in the city, the core of life remains simple: we are born and we die. And within that short space of life we are to find the Truth — what it was all about.

Jesus Christ is the Truth. Therefore, if you would wield the sword of the Lord, speak — or write — Christ.

Truly yours,

Jonathan Woodman

ATTILA D. HUNN, D.D.S.
Canal Route #3
Toledo, Ohio

September 25

Dear Mr. Versteeg,

I don't appreciate your characterizing the dental bills your parents incurred for you when you were a youngster as "staggering."

In the interest of fairness, you might at least have explained that when you were young your teeth decayed simply when oxygen touched them, and that your doting parents sent you for almost weekly repair to Cincinnati's most expensive dentist on the theory that more expensive was better.

Now you're biting the hand that filled your teeth.

I don't notice you quibbling about money when you come in here with an emergency problem.

If you'll figure your dental bills per bite and chew, you'll see that you never had such a bargain.

But what's really ironic is that you can still have incisors left in your mouth while, as far as I can see, you have got yourself a toothless religion.

When is the last time you bit into a really tough social issue? What about the poor and dispossessed? What about the oppressed and disenfranchised?

It's pretty hard for me to swallow a religion that doesn't bite into problems of social injustice.

You still need to learn to put your money where your mouth is.

Sincerely,

Attila D. Hunn, D.D.S.

P.S. May we please have something on your account?

362636 Starlet Drive
Hollywood, California

September 29

Dear V.,

I've been thinning.
So far so good. I'm using those appetite-suppressant pills. Supposed to control your appetite. Eat less — *slim!*
And I've been thinking how neat it would be if someone would also invent pills to suppress some of our other appetites.
How 'bout a pill to suppress pride's hunger for self-aggrandizement — getting fat on flattery, always needing to be right, always needing to fill out our puffed-up self-image?
How 'bout a pill to harness the power drive — eaten up with envy and stuffing ourselves with authority?
How 'bout a pill to deaden our mammon pangs, control our greed, and free us from our self-destructive selfishness?
Most of all, we could use a pill to stop our desire and taste for blood and revenge, our insatiable appetite for violence and brutality. If we keep on indulging such appetites, we'll gorge ourselves to death, and the rest of the world, too.
The Gospel can make us free and it's not a bitter pill to swallow.

Luv a Bunch!

Gloria Glitz

MANNY'S GYM
Four Seasons Drive
Toledo, Ohio

October 2

Hey, Rev,

You know it's fall when them brown things fall outa the sky — footballs.

The fall of the year don't mean fallin leaves as much as fallin fullbacks.

An when we are outa daylight savin time an need to remember to set our clocks we say fall backward, we are ignorin some of the greatest advice any guy ever give: Fall forward.

It is inrevetible that as you go through life you are gonna get stopped. You hardly never run the kick-off back all the way.

It's normal to push toward your goal — get stopped. Try again — get tackled. Try again. That's another great lesson football teaches about life — you gotta keep tryin, no matter how often you get blocked or knocked on your whatsis.

But the thing every great fullback knows is to get ever inch you can by fallin forward.

Honest now — you ain't never noticed how a goal post looks like a cross?

Your pal,

Hulk Hagarson

4246 Rose Point Court
Toledo, Ohio

October 4

Dear Rev. Bob,

Being your neighbor down the street, I could scarcely fail to notice that you and a group from the church were redecorating the parsonage this past week. In fact, since the drapes were down, I was practically forced to observe the entire process.

And frankly, I found it inspirational. Off came that crazy wallpaper; on went gallons and gallons of paint, a bit of new wallpaper, and *voila!* I must say your place is greatly improved.

Before you do put the new drapes up, I thought I should tell you just how inspired I am.

I've been thinking that maybe I ought to redecorate my personality.

I've got some sticky old grudges that have been covering the walls of my soul for years. Now that I look at them, I see that they're grimy and frayed at the corners. I really would like to get rid of them and brighten things up a bit.

Some new paint — maybe a bit of sunshine yellow, or peaceful white, or even an accent of joyful red — that's just what I want to live in through the winter coming on. I'm going to get right to work at it.

Your sermons haven't gotten me going, but your work crew has!

Sincerely,

A. Nabor

P. S. Did you have to work on Sunday?

666 Shoehorn Manor
Toledo, Ohio

October 6

Versteeg:

It's not bad enough you can't get people to come to church; now you're trying to get them to go to the movies instead.

I'm mighty glad I made up my mind not to give that church one red cent while you are the so-called minister there, because I would hate to think that some of my hard-earned money went to pay for mailing out advertising for a movie!

It's a cushy job you've got, with nothing better to do than go to the movies!

Movies are made by people who snort cocaine and get divorced or worse. Movies are the Devil's tail.

Why don't you get busy and try to help people to lead holy lives?

What do you think the church is, anyway — a party?

Offended,

Henrietta Peckingham

362636 Starlet Drive
Hollywood, California

October 8

Dear V.,

This movie I've got a bit part in — for the climax it's got the neatest scene.

The Good Guy and the Bad Guy are locked in this air-tight room that's filling with leaking gas. Each of them has got a pistol and they're aiming at each other.

If either one of them fires his pistol, the whole building — and everybody else in it — will explode.

Scary, huh?

Just like the world.

As long as the premise is that there are Good Guys and Bad Guys (we know who is who), that they have to be enemies, and they have loaded weapons armed and aimed, everyone is in danger of the scariest kind. And it's no movie.

How can we re-define the situation and see the other not as a threat but as a potential — more, a necessary — ally in managing the real threat?

No, I don't know how the script works out. I've only read my part.

Life is easier on a sound stage where the only actual blowups are temperamental.

In the real world we have to write our own parts to make it work out.

We're all in this air-tight room, see. . .

Luv a Bunch!

Glori Glitz

Heart of the Forest
Black Mountain
North Carolina

October 9

Dear Bob,

I have been watching the trees change in the forest.
In my mind an old hymn played counterpoint:
Change and decay in all around I see.
O Thou who changest not, abide with me.
Maybe God changest not, but he surely calls us to change
— the kind of change which may be another name, not for
decay, but for growth.

God calls us to grow, and the change may be beautiful —
from glory to glory.

And though we appear to be as grass which withers, the
reality is that, rooted and grounded in love, we shall be like a
tree planted by the waters of life.

Changeably yours,

Jonathan Woodman

RABBIT RUN VOLKSWAGON INC.
13 Upshaft Drive
Toledo, Ohio

October 12

Pastor Vorshtag:

I regret, but, yes, it is necessary to make adjustments to the fuel-injection system of your Volkswagen. The engine is racing, burning up gasoline, and putting unnecessary wear on its components.

I hope you will not think I am being unduly personal when I say that I have observed you in our Customer Waiting Area while we worked on your automobile, and in my opinion, your own engine is racing too much, too, Pastor Vorshtag.

You need to adjust so that, when it is necessary to idle, you can idle without putting wear and tear on your system.

Why don't you carry a book or learn to meditate? Then, when you get in a traffic jam in the two most likely places — the beltline or the express lane at the grocery — instead of racing your engine you could put yourself in neutral, idle efficiently, not waste fuel, and not wear yourself out.

'Wiedersehen!

Wolfgang von Krankcase
Service Manager

ATILLA D. HUNN

ATTILA D. HUNN, D.D.S.
Canal Route #3
Toledo, Ohio

October 13

Dear Mr. Versteeg,

Now that's a laugh — you telling me that you can't stand Horrid Cosell's mouth.

How can you argue with success? Horrid Cosell is the most successful mouth in the country.

Your problem is that you can't stand perfection. Horrid Cosell is perfect.

Horrid Cosell knows by heart every punch in every combination that Muhammed Ali ever threw — and when and where and against whom — and he knows what Granny Rice's Great Aunt Lulu said about it.

Horrid Cosell knows how many blades of grass the middle front cleat of Dandy Don's right shoe tore up on the seventh pass he threw at 2:41-to-go in the second quarter when the Dallas Cowboys crushed the Minnesota Vikings 27 to 17 on November 11, 1968.

Horrid Cosell knows that Sandy Koufax wiggled his left eyebrow twice before he made the second pick-off throw in the third game of his second Series, but the runner, Frank Robinson, whose cousin Adelbert was eating a mint-chocolate-chip cone in seat 37-W of the left-field bleachers at the moment, was back in plenty of time, touching base with the little toe of his right foot while. . .

Horrid Cosell sees all, knows all, tells all.

Being perfect himself, Horrid Cosell is in a position to perform the valuable function of pointing out the shortcomings of the rest of the world.

Of course, no one has ever seen Horrid Cosell himself so much as fling a Frisbee or knuckle an agate — or even try to — much less bat a ball or block a linebacker. That makes Horrid Cosell the perfect sportscaster, the spectator-talker par excellence.

Meredith and Gifford, on the other hand, are handicapped: they started out as mere doers, and therein they had to expose their own fallibilities. Like all doers, they made mistakes — of which Total-Recall Horrid frequently reminds them with an implacably sadistic ghoulishness.

Frankly, Mr. Versteeg, I wonder if your inability to take a shine to Horrid Cosell isn't just plain and simple professional jealousy.

Horrid Cosell talks about things people like listening to because they can listen to Horrid and, like Horrid, not have to do anything. You preachers, on the other hand, talk about God's love which moves us to respond in faith — to become ourselves doers as well as hearers.

Having looked into both, I give it as my professional opinion, Mr. Versteeg, that Horrid Cosell's mouth is in a lot better shape than your own.

Sincerely,

Attila D. Hunn, D.D.S.

P.S. May we please have something on your account?

Heart of the Forest
Black Mountain
North Carolina

October 16

Dear Bob,

I had to visit the city to see a sick friend. One thing I noticed while in the city was how much more the dogs bark there than they do in the forest.

Here in the forest, a dog will bark because there's something strange about, because he wants your attention, or because he wants to hear a reassuring sound.

In the city, I think, dogs bark because they're nervous. They must be nervous a lot.

And then I noticed that in the city the people bark, too, and I think for the same reason. But the more they bark, it seems, the more nervous everyone gets.

Do you think there's anything you can do to help people in the city bark less?

Truly yours,

Jonathan Woodman

MANNY'S GYM
Four Seasons Drive
Toledo, Ohio

October 17

Hey, Rev,

Hows come you ain't preachin no World Serious sermons?

You know how in the Book of Ax it says how Saint Paul seen all them Greek shrines an he said in his sermon, "I seen youse is very religious an got a shrine to The Unknown God an I am gonna tell youse who He is."

Well, Rev, if you wanna know what shrine folks today is really worshippin at, I tell you Take Me Out To The Old Ball Game an you oughta be tellin 'em who is the Greatest Manager of 'em all.

You are missin a good bunt.

For example, you could preach about the guy what tries to send his wife up to bat for him at church as his D.H. ony there ain't no D.H.es allowed in this year's World Serious.

You could preach about the guy what wants his World Serious ring when he ain't never even made spring trainin or showed up to play in even one game. An you could preach about the pinch hitter who gets his full pay even though he come in in the last inning an swung the bat ony oncet.

An you could preach about how to handle a unfair call what goes against you.

An you could preach about hittin with a 3-2 count how it ony takes one.

An you could preach about playin your assigned position an how it takes all sorts of talent.

You don't have to thank me for these here ideas, Rev. You could even sell hot dogs.

World Seriously Your Pal,

Hulk Hagarson

26 Steinem Square
Toledo, Ohio

19 October

Rev. Ms. or Sir:

I find it hard to believe that you are World Seriously watching that baseball farce on tv.

The entire thing is a chauvinist charade.

Out of fifty so-called athletes — not to mention trainers, coaches, and personagers — not one is a woperson.

Who are the females in the World Series? They are the players' wives sitting in the stands, glimpsed in REDBOOK camera shots, blowing the whistle for (not on), clapping, cheering, admiring their Big, Brave, Bold Men of Action out on the Diamond Doing Something!

And they are the Cute Little Chicks who police the pigpen (they call it "bullpen"!), sashaying after foul balls which they meekly surrender up into the stands.

And you — a person of the cloth — have the gall to waste your time watching this slop! I'll bet you go to topless bars and burlesque shows, too — Baldy!

I thought you were supposed to be a dedicated servant of all hupersonity, both male and female.

Most stupid of all, you don't see that this is one more ploy in Kapitalism's Bread-and-Circuses slavery.

This world is burning with oppression, hunger, tyranny, and greed, and there you are, fiddling with the fine tuner.

You claim it's just wholesome recreation, huh? OK; now how about a little recreation of the fallen social order? You going to spend twenty hours now paying attention to world hunger? Or isn't that as serious as the Series?

You going to give for the ministry of your church as much as you spend — or bet — on baseball and other pastimes?

I'm waiting for your next pitch, Preach, and I'm going to pound it right up your middle.

Sororitarily,

Ms. Jill Jockey

THE NEON PALM
Miami, Florida

October 24

Dear Mr. Versteeg,

So the temporary crown on your molar has come off for the third time. So why are you excited? Am I excited?

I'm surprised at you. In your profession you are always telling others that all earthly crowns are only temporary, are subject to being lost, and that the crown of life comes only to those who are faithful unto death.

Therefore, when I do get back to put in your permanent crown, you must not confuse *permanant* with *eternal*.

But you surely can't expect me to come all the way back from Miami for one tooth — yours. I'll have a look at it as soon as I'm back in town.

Meanwhile my advice is; Don't bite off more than you can chew.

Attentively,

Attila D. Hunn, D.D.S.

P.S. May we please have something on your account?

362636 Starlet Drive
Hollywood, California

October 25

Dear V.,

Because of the headlines, I've been remembering the time we did Irwin Shaw's play, *Bury the Dead* — when the slain soldiers refuse to lie down in their graves to be buried.

You remember how we began that production with a dumb show of the squad of soldiers tracing the evolution of battle weapons from Stone Age to Nuclear Age, and then ending up dead but unburied.

Next time, we won't be able to bury the dead.

If we have weapons, we use weapons.

History has it no other way.

The way to limit and eradicate war is to limit and eradicate weapons.

In our day, the weapons go, or we go.

No nukes!

Luv a Bunch!

Glori Glitz

MANNY'S GYM
Four Seasons Drive
Toledo, Ohio

October 27

Hey, Rev,

I saw them Olympics gymnastics finals.

I thought maybe I was gonna like the rings or the high bar the best, or maybe even the uneven parable bars or the balance beam. But you know what it turns out I like best?

The floor exercise.

Man, that's a pure sport.

Ony equipment is the human body. It's great!

It made me think about our graceful life — I mean life what has been touched by grace.

It ain't how much equipment you got to monkey aroun with; it's the pure style of how you live — that's what counts.

Movin through life with grace — that's really livin in style!

A perfect ten!

Your Pal,

Hulk Hagarson

ARMIN LEGG, M.D.

ARMIN LEGG, M. D.
Asthma Plaza
1998 Humerus Highway
Toledo, Ohio

October 29

Dear Reverend Versteeg,

All our test data show no organic cause for your fatigued leg muscles. Running 10 K a day should be no problem under ordinary circumstances.

I suggest that no matter how inclement the weather or how inconvenient it may be for you to find time during daylight, you should nevertheless do your running cross country, out of doors. Whatever you do, stop running indoors at the YMCA.

The object of running for fun should be self-improvement, not competition.

But you obviously cannot stand to have a body in front of you on that indoor track. You feel you have to catch up with all the others and pass them. Holden Caufield has nothing on you when it comes to misunderstanding: you want to be the catcher in the Y.

And once you pass someone on that little YMCA track, lo and behold! There they appear in front of you again, and you think you again have to catch and pass them. So you go on running your level Sisyphus race.

I prescribe for you a dose of St. Paul: stop running around in little circles trying to catch everything in front of you which as soon as you pass it, turns out to be in front of you again. Instead just run the course that is set before you with patience.

For your good health,

Armin Legg, M.D.

P.S. I'll bet I'm less competitive than you are.

50 Hugenot Drive
Toledo, Ohio

October 31

Dear Rev. Versteeg,

Because I don't want the embarrassment of having to tell you this myself, I'm asking someone else to write this letter to you.

We had hoped to bring our Youth Group to sing for you last Sunday, but as I am job hunting and had the opportunity for an out-of-town job interview last Sunday, I had to postpone our appearance at your church to this coming Sunday.

Well, unfortunately the same thing has happened again: I have another interview opportunity this coming Sunday, so we must cancel our appearance with you this Sunday, too.

Sorry to disappoint you. We know you would have enjoyed our Youth — for whom this has been a great learning adventure.

Sincerely,

Marie Saulterre

P.S. I'm looking for letters of reference to support my resume. If you can see your way clear to writing a note emphasizing my dependability, I would appreciate it.

RABBIT RUN VOLKSWAGON INC.
13 Upshaft Drive
Toledo, Ohio

November 3

Pastor Vorshtag:

I am regretful to hear you complain because we put a new set of sparkplugs in your automobile.

The fact that you had just had them replaced six weeks before is really beside the points.

After all, you do a great deal of city driving; you use regular gasoline; and those plugs were made in America.

How many weeks do you expect a parishioner to go on one sermon? Maybe if your points were cleaner, your parishioners would get better mileage.

If, according to you, spiritual tune-ups are needed every day, how can you complain about new spark plugs every six weeks?

'Wiedersehen!

Wolfgang von Krankcase
Service Manager

MANNY'S GYM
Four Seasons Drive
Toledo, Ohio

November 5

Hey, Rev,

Lemme see have I got this right?

Reason Methodists call their annual meetin a "Charge Conference" is because oncet upon a time a "charge" was a church or group of churches that a Pastor was appointed to have "charge" of, huh?

What I wanna know is does that mean he was supposed to be "in charge" (which clearly you ain't), or as they usta say "charged with the responsibility of"? You know — like that hymn: "A charge to keep I have"?

Because I thought maybe it was a "charge" like a rifle cartridge has got that makes the bullet go, an in that case I know some churches that have been keepin their charge for a long time.

Or I thought maybe it was a "charge" like in "Like a mighty army moves the church of God," in which case ditto.

Then I got to thinkin maybe it was a "charge" like them churches I heard about that are takin Mastercard, or some church members who figure the church can just charge everything an forget it.

I was really hopin it might be a conference like you could get your battries charged up from.

Or better still, like a football team when a take-charge quarterback comes in. Man! that's the kinda Mastercharge I'd like to see — when the Master would come in an take charge of the church!

Outta that I would get a charge.

Your Pal,

Hulk Hagarson

Heart of the Forest
Black Mountain
North Carolina

November 7

Dear Bob,

Most of my forest, you remember, is evergreen, but as they shed their leaves, the elms I do have open up now to skies turning grey.

I've been cutting firewood. I can hardly wait for the cool to come so I can build my fire.

Cold has already come up there where you live in the north, hasn't it? But you have no fireplace this year?

How will you ever make it through the winter without a fireplace?

The warmth of open flame, the smell of burning wood, the crackling, the changing, living glow of the breathing fire — how will you make it through the winter without them?

No fireplace! Columbia Gas, you say? I don't understand. It seems sad.

I understand why Moses saw God as a bush afire, and I understand why the Holy Spirit descended to the disciples as tongues of fire. Elijah notwithstanding, God speaks to me in the fire. Am I guilty of a Zoroastrian heresy?

I hope you are not going to be like people who once upon a time were warmed in the glow of the Gospel, but who now have moved away from it and try to warm themselves instead by the mechanisms of a materialistic technology. It isn't the same, is it?

They'll never be satisfied and warm until they get close to the Burning Bush again.

I wish you many happy bonfires this winter. When you enjoy them — warm outside in the cold — think of your warm friend, and I'll think of you warmly.

Truly yours,

Jonathan Woodman

362636 Starlet Drive
Hollywood, California

November 9

Dear V.,

First thing I do when I get home from the grocery store is start a new grocery list.

Before I get this bagful put away in the cupboard, I've thought of something else I'm almost out of.

It used to irritate me, but now I look at it in a different way.

I remember hearing about a man who kept complaining about how much money his son cost him — prenatal doctors' bills, delivery, pediatricians, clothes, dentists, toys, food, schooling, this, that, and the other thing — until one sad day the young man was killed and hasn't cost the father a dime since.

As long as we still need things, it means we're still alive, and what good are things, including money, except to sustain and enrich life?

So I complain less about the never-ending need for things and money. That's *life!*

Luv a Bunch!

Gloria Glitz

666 Shoehorn Manor
Toledo, Ohio

November 12

Versteeg:

You have got a nerve, sending me a pledge card!

I certainly have no intention of supporting that church:
What has that church done for me?

I was in that church last Easter, before you came here.
I've been waiting ever since. Do you suppose the minister has
come to call? Not on your tin-type.

You'd think someone would have missed me by now. Cousin Clarabelle tells me I should phone the church and tell you
I want a visit, but I think any minister worth his salt would
have wondered where I was and figured it out for himself by
now.

I'm awful lonesome, I'll tell you. If it weren't for my tele-
phone and my shopping trips and my son stopping by on his
way home from work, and my euchre club and the country
club, I wouldn't see hardly anyone.

And now you want money from me to help support a
minister who, as far as I can tell, runs around town, plays tennis, and listens to Horrid Cosell? Forget it.

My advice to you is: Stop wasting our money supporting tv
ministry, ecumenism, hospitals and homes, and hunger cru-
sades and missions and evangelism and education and youth
retreats and all your other fancy-dancy programs and high-
falutin' meetings and doings, and pay more attention to real
people like me.

Until you do, not a cent.

Determinedly,

Henrietta Peckingham

50 Hugenot Drive
Toledo, Ohio

November 14

Dear Rev. Versteeg,

I'm sorry, but I cannot give you any money for the church this year.

You know how sick I've been. You remember how the doctors gave me up for dead and said it would take a miracle from God to save me and how all the people at the church were praying for me.

And then I spent two months in the hospital getting well.

And now I have all these medical bills to pay, so I don't have any money left over for the Lord.

I know you'll understand.

Sincerely,

Marie Saulterre

22 Turnabout Lane
Toledo, Ohio

November 17

Dear Rev. Vestige,

I am enclosing $50.00 for last quarter of year.
And wish to send $50.00 each quarter next year.
I will not sign a pledge card but I will give what I did this year.

Sincerely,

Lottie Stannard

711 Easy Street
Toledo, Ohio

November 18

Dear Pastor Verstug,

Not this year, I'm afraid.

Things are going great — no problems. Best year we've ever had, in spite of the economy.

Things are going so well for me that I've had no need at all for any of the church's services, and since I haven't had to call on the church, I don't see why the church should call on me.

I take the automatic deduction for charities, anyway, so I don't have to itemize.

Maybe under next year's tax structure it'll be different.

Sincerely,

Holden Fast

362636 Starlet Drive
Hollywood, California

November 21

Dear V.,

Hey, you're comin' down heavy.

Some of us are poverty types and literally don't have any money to give to the church. We feel bad enough about it without you getting on our case.

But I am willing to tithe my time and talent.

I'm willing to work four hours a week at my church out here — stuffing envelopes, cleaning up, and so on.

I teach an exercise class for our church ladies, and I'm going to direct the Christmas pageant.

I know that our church has bills that have to be paid and a program that has to be financed; and I know that there are people who need to be helped to grow to carry their fair share.

All the same, lighten up, huh?

Luv a Bunch!

Gloria Glitz

Limestone Collegiate Church
Fort Industry Square
Toledo, Ohio

November 25

Dear Brother Versteeg,

I happen to know that your church has many members who can't afford to give money.

I also know one who crochets pillows, sells the pillows, and gives that money to the church.

People who have that kind of spirit know what giving is all about.

We can learn from them.

Fraternally,

Rev. I. Rant

Dictated by Dr. Rant, but signed in his absence.

666 Shoehorn Manor
Toledo, Ohio

November 26

Versteeg:

How dare you send that lackey around here asking for my pledge!

I've got problems of my own.

The Thanksgiving turkey I bought was too big to fit in the oven, so I had to go out and buy a bigger oven.

Murphy was right: nothing ever works out.

I sure don't have any money left for the likes of you.

One turkey is enough. Too much.

The trouble with you preachers is you're always begging for money.

Get stuffed.

Henrietta Peckingham

HENRIETTA
PECKINGHAM

Aldersgate Lane
Toledo, Ohio

November 28

Dear Pastor Bob,

I want to increase my partnership with the Lord.
My pledge card's enclosed.

Sincerely,

John Pilgrim

WINTER

JAZZY CAROLS
AND MUDDY CLEATS

58

3015 Scottwood Avenue
Toledo, Ohio

November 29

Dear Pastor Bob,

This is the day after Thanksgiving, and I just got the Advent Offering Folder in the mail. I don't understand it.

An advent offering of twenty-five cents a day, I can understand.

Self-denial I can understand.

What I can't understand is the connection between an offering of a lousy quarter a day and any kind of self-denial. Especially after the way I stuffed my face yesterday.

If the food for that feast had cost $9.50 more than it did, I would have paid it without blinking. According to the folder you sent, $9.50 is what I'll come up with after thirty-eight days of self-denial.

Hey, Versteeg? What is this malarkey?

Yours,

Gordon Glutz*

---

*Gordon's letter came to me by way of The Rev. Howard Abts, who says he has no idea how the letter got misdelivered to him.

362636 Starlet Drive
Hollywood, California

December 1

Dear V.,

Everybody out here in Burbank — Hollywood — is talented, specially talented. The talents run the gamut.
And the competition is awesome.
Some people dance better than I do, sing better than I do, look better than I do, and (I know you'll find this hard to believe) even act better than I do.
I don't really mind all that. I even enjoy it.
But career-wise, there is the problem of Sticking It Out. And personal-wise, there is the question I have to take home with me after a day of rejections: What makes me so Special?
Then I remember what makes me special:
God gave himself to me; Jesus gave himself for me — for every one else, too — and that makes me and everyone else special.
Nothing diminishes my own specialness which doesn't come from me, but comes to me from the Lord's love.
This Christmas I wish you what you have wished me: May Your Star Shine!

Luv a Bunch!

Gloria Glitz

RABBIT RUN VOLKSWAGON INC.
13 Upshaft Drive
Toledo, Ohio

December 3

Pastor Vorshtag:

I am regretful that you feel overcharged for repair of the cranking mechanism of your Volkswagen's driver-side window.

Consider what an important part of your automobile the window crank is and how much it means to you.

The window crank permits adjustment to changing meteorological conditions; it permits operation of hospital parking gates; and, it permits drive-through purchasing of hamburgers.

Historically, the earliest automobiles had no windows and the drivers had no such options. Today your automobile has eight windows, two of which can be adjusted — that is, admittedly, when the cranking mechanism works.

What would your automobile be like, Pastor Vorshtag, if you could not keep out the cold in winter or let in the fresh air in the spring? It would be like a rigid personality who cannot protect himself when people are cold or — even worse — cannot open up to the new wind blowing when people are warm. One must learn to do both.

Doktors sometimes refer to their patients by their case names. Here at the garage we refer to you as The Window Crank.

'Wiedersehen!

Wolfgang von Krankcase
Service Manager

MANNY'S GYM
Four Seasons Drive
Toledo, Ohio

December 5

Hey, Rev,

Bout them used tires.

I seen lotsa diffrunt things done with em.

I got em in my back yard. They're part of my obstacle course, in two rows together, an ya run through em with high choppy steps.

I got one of em on a rope from a tree an I throw the ball through it. Oncet I found the neighbor's kid swingin in it. Ain't nothin sacred no more?

Remember when we put a bunch of em under that homemade landin pad Rusty usta pole vault into?

Then when I was runnin by the school the other day, I seen a bunch of em laid out on the playground to mark outta bounds for a playin field.

When I joined the church, I hadda make a four-wheel promise. I promist I'd support the church with my (1) prayers, my (2) gifts, my (3) service, an my (4) attendance.

Sometimes I've gone a little flat on one or other of them four wheel promises.

So every Padre oughta figure out some way to use all them wore-out tires he's got lyin aroun.

You tell me. What can the Lord do with a wore-out promise? Retread?

Your pal,

Hulk Hagarson

666 Shoehorn Manor
Toledo, Ohio

December 6

Versteeg:

I heard you preached a sermon about that beeper you carry when you're a chaplain at the hospital. Be nice if just once you'd get a sermon out of the Bible.

What is this stuff about the Manger being God's paging device calling us to answer the cries of the needy?

I mean I'm really tired of hearing about your anti-Christmas sermons. What are you — Scrooge in an alb?

I hope that come Christmas Eve I get reports that you've shaped up and started preaching the true Christmas message — the angels and the shepherds and the baby Jesus and Silent Night and White Christmas.

And lay off the politics. Why can't you be more like Reverend Fallgood and just preach the Gospel?

I only hope you haven't just ruined Christmas for everybody.

Boy, I'd like to beep your beeper!

Forthrightly for the true
Christmas spirit,

Henrietta Peckingham

362636 Starlet Drive
Hollywood, California

December 8

Dear V.,

Started Christmas shopping — can't wait: love it!
Bought my nephews twin books: STORIES FROM THE BI-
BLE and FAIRY TALES.

They go together. Know how?

They're twin mirrors.

Fairy tales — I mean, like all art — are the mirror in
which we see the image of our human nature.

Of course, there's a lot of great art in the Bible, too,
but there's something more: the Bible is also the mirror
in which we see the image of God.

Isn't the Gospel of Jesus Christ that those two im-
ages come together at last when the image of God is restored in persons through Jesus?

Bruno Bettelheim (I love cute names!) says:

> Whatever may be true in reality, the child who
> listens to fairy tales comes to imagine and believe
> that out of love for him his parent is willing to risk his
> life to bring him the present he most desires. In his
> turn, such a child believes that he is worthy of such
> devotion, because he would be willing to sacrifice his
> life out of love for his parent. Thus the child will grow
> up to bring peace and happiness even to those who
> are so grievously afflicted that they seem like beasts.
> In so doing, a person will gain happiness for himself
> and his life's partner and, with it, happiness also for
> his parents. He will be at peace with himself and the
> world.*

Bruno Bettelheim, *The Uses of Enchantment,* Alfred A. Knopf, New York, 1976,
p. 310.

That's no fairy tale; that's the Gospel truth.

Luv a Bunch!

Gloria Glitz

Heart of the Forest
Black Mountain
North Carolina

December 9

Dear Bob,

The Christmas season has opened here in the forest and
I'm a little nervous. Christmas season is also hunting season.
So far two deer have been shot and three hunters.
I imagine that in the city the Christmas hunt probably
kills more than that — hunting for a gift for Aunt Martha,
hunting for bargains, hunting for time to get everything done,
hunting for a parking space, hunting for a way to lose the
holiday avoirdupois, hunting for a way out of debt, hunting
for some real meaning in it all.
You could get lost in the city's Christmas rushes easier
than you can get lost here in the woods.
Some lose Christ.
And there he is, hunting for us.
Not to kill, but to reclaim.

Christmas Joy to you
and yours!

Jonathan Woodman

P.S. I put the suet on your Christmas tree for the birds.

3/4 Tyme Street
Toledo, Ohio

December 10

Dear Rev. Versicle,

We find the fact that your **Ministerial Association** will not allow choirs from non-Ministerial-Association-member churches to sing in your **Advent Carol Service** most un-Christmas-like.

Our church does not belong to the Ministerial Association because we do not believe in ecumenicity.

But if you do not let us take part in your Christmas sing, how ecumenical are *you?*

Puzzled,

Carol A. Long

362636 Starlet Drive
Hollywood, California

December 11

Dear V.,

Trying to catch something of the Christmas spirit out here in Tinsel Town, we drove the other day down to San Juan de Capistrano to look at the Christmas decorations.

The life-size *creche* looked so special with the shepherd figures kneeling there that I decided to kneel down beside them, but there was a fence between us, so it kinda lacked something.

At first I assumed that the fence was to keep the tourists from playing dog in the manger; but then I got to wondering if maybe the fence was there, not to keep us out, but to keep the Christ Child in.

Unlike Bethlehem's inn, today we really do have a place for Jesus, and we intend to keep him in his place — safely (for us) inside the pretty picture.

He wasn't crucified because he was born in a manger, but because he grew up and got out to be bold in the temple and challenging in the marketplace and peaceable in the Pentagon ('scuse me: back then they called it the Praetorium, didn't they?).

Then I heard the music. How smart God is to set the Christmas story to music! They can't fence in the music.

As I knelt beside the fence with the shepherds and the Holy Family figures on the other side, the Christmas spirit came out to me on the wings of song and caught me.

Try to contain him as we will, he really is a free spirit, isn't he?

Luv a Bunch!

Gloria Glitz

Heart of the Forest
Black Mountain
North Carolina

December 12

Dear Bob,

We're having our Advent Choir Festival here in the forest, too.

The birds and squirrels and other woodland singers chorus along my path in the morning chill, and I join them with a whistle or a hum.

Singing together is one of the best things we can do.

Who sing together I think God can bring together.

When we sing together, we follow the good impulse of the Christmas story: "there was with the angel a multitude of the heavenly host praising God and saying" — and we all feel they were saying it with song — "Glory to God in the highest, and on earth peace, good will toward men."

It is the New Creation's echo of that first creation: "When the morning stars sang together, and all the children of God shouted for joy."

Join the Christmas chorus!

On the upbeat!

Truly yours,

Jonathan

ATTILA D. HUNN, D.D.S.
Canal Route #3
Toledo, Ohio

December 13

Dear Mr. Versteeg,

Knowing that your strength to resist temptation comes in at something about the level of a straw's ability to balance on a knife-edge in a hurricane, I write to remind you again this year to lay off the Christmas candy.

Candy rots your teeth, Mr. Versteeg. I cannot help you if you make your teeth rot.

You need to stick to nourishing food — period.

And while I'm at it, let me remind you that if you go in for the Christmas "sweets" spiritually — I mean if you sentimentalize about Christmas (and to "sentimentalize about Christmas" means to get on a gooey glow and then do nothing about letting the living Christ into your daily living) — if, I say, you suck on Christmas sweets instead of feeding your soul real Christmas nourishment, what you rot is your soul.

Happy Holidays!

Sincerely,

Attila D. Hunn, D.D.S.

P.S. May we please have something on your account?

One and Two Downbeat
Street
Ann Arbor, Michigan

December 14

V.,

So I went to hear the ol' man Dave Brubeck hisself play his FIESTA DE LA POSADA an' it was all right.

Piano players has got a right to celebrate Christmas, too.

Second half the concert was Brubeck an' two of his kids an' a harmonica player gettin' down some mean music.

Las' encore they play is great an' not until the las' three measures does this dude sittin' next ta me recognize they are playin' a jazz version of "Jingle Bells."

Ever tune in on the fact some folks don't recognize the Lord's songs because some of his angels sing jazz?

Have one, man.

Joe Kuhl

Santa's Sweat Shop
North Pole
December 15

Dear Bobby John,

Thank you for your card. You're right. This being our
busy season, I have little time to write, not that I'm sure you
can understand the answer anyway. But I'll try. Lord knows I
try.

My job is the same as always: I hide Christmas in presents.

While all the others around here are making the gifts —
cutting out, sawing up, nailing together, painting, wrapping
— my job is to slip around and hide the Christmas spirit
among the presents. Something like the folks who drop premi-
ums in cereal boxes, except I do it secretly.

No, I don't hide Christmas in each and every present.
Some get by me, others I wouldn't touch with a ten-foot North
Pole.

Sometimes I hide Christmas in a present as a gentle
thought cherished all year long. Sometimes I hide it as a deep
concern that shapes a life. Sometimes I hide it as a happy
sacrifice — mostly in gifts that cost very little in dollar terms,
say, a widow's mite. Sometimes I hide it as a prayer for the
recipient's health and happiness.

When you've been at the job as long as I have, you know
hundreds of ways.

But millions on earth never see the Christmas secret buried under the piles of gifts. Many discard it with the tags.

You'd be surprised how many never find the Christmas in
their gifts. Yet life is full of it unseen, as bread is full of yeast.
'Must run now.

Season's Greetings!

Elvin

P.S. Thanks again for your card. Did you forget to put in this
year's check? I didn't find it. 'Thought maybe it was an
oversight.

666 Shoehorn Manor
Toledo, Ohio

December 17

Versteeg:

All around me at Christmas time I see evidence of your in-
competence — you and all the rest of those effete ineffectuals
who have gone and gotten yourselves ordained ministers.

Have you been out in the real world? It's a jungle. I mean
shopping.

I've had my eye on some special material to make my holiday tablecloth for my parties. Do you know they want $8.95 a
yard for it? Can you imagine! I'll croak first.

Then there was a sale on a perfectly darling dress I would
have looked stunning in at our Club dance, but some hen-
naed hussy practically tore it out of my hands and bought it.
If I could have held on with two hands she wouldn't have gotten it, but I couldn't drop my other armload, could I? In that
dress she'll look like an overcooked plum. Serves her right!

I went to the bargain store sale to get something for my
euchre club's gift exchange, and the mob at the tables was
like a pack of sharks around bloody meat. I had to nudge my
elbows raw before I was able to get ten and a half matched
pairs of potholders, and my umbrella got bent!

I did find a lovely pair of shoes — just what I've been
looking for and a real bargain. I'm sure they got put back in
the wrong box and that new sales clerk didn't know the difference, so I got them at almost half what I think they were supposed to be — a steal. To make it perfect, the Dumb Dora
miscounted the change and gave me fifty cents more than she
was supposed to!

But when I went to buy a little Scotch for Christmas Eve,
the clerk in the store was downright surly. That's what happens when state employees have a monopoly.

I could give you more examples, but I trust I've made my
point.

It's pretty obvious, isn't it, that people today just don't

have the Christmas spirit.

And it's pretty obvious, isn't it, whose fault that is?
You preachers sure are letting us down.

Forthrightly,

Henrietta Peckingham

GLORIA GLITZ

362636 Starlet Drive
Hollywood, California

December 20

Dear V.,

This Christmas I'm intrigued by *creches.*
There's the baby Jesus — a tiny doll.
Remember that old movie where Lionel Barrymore was the villain in drag, turning all those people into dolls? In our age of miniaturization, it seems that in lots of peoples' Christmas Jesus is infinitesimal — they barely notice him at all.

On the other hand, I feel like that lady who said she couldn't understand Oral's vision of a three-football-field-high Jesus because her Bible and her experience gave her visions of a Jesus who cared about little things — grains of mustard seed, sparrows, widow's mites.

I guess the question about our Christmas vision of Christ is not whether it makes us bigger or smaller, but whether it makes us more like Jesus or less.

But as far as that vision's concerned, whenever we make him the incredible shrinking Christ, we make ourselves the incredible shrinking souls.

Merry, Happy, and
Luv a Bunch!

Glori Glitz

Everywhere-and-Here

25 December

Dear Child,

I am giving you for Christmas the costliest and most precious gift ever given: I am giving you myself.

My gift is above the like gift from any other because I am above any other, Alpha and Omega, the pre-existent source of all other existence.

There is no question of my ability to give you this gift, for I am Grace itself.

Only in question is your own ability to make room for me, to open your heart and life, to receive.

Peace and Good Will!

With Love,

Father

Heart of the Forest
Black Mountain
North Carolina

December 29

Dear Bob,

Thank you for your Christmas letter.

Sorry about the trouble with your car. What is an "alternator"?

Christmas here in the forest was quiet but busy.

We had our Christmas feast — bread for the birds and
oats for the animals.

Popcorn and cranberries decked the tree which was be-
comingly modest but obviously pleased to be chosen as this
year's Christmas tree.

I read aloud the Christmas story from the New Testament. We acted out the angels' appearance to the shepherds
and the Wise Men's journey. I lit a candle. I sang *Silent
Night.*

I opened my eyes to behold my gifts from God: the trees,
the sky, the sun and moon and stars, the snow, the stream,
my home, my food, my fire, my body, my friends, and, of
course most of all, the gift of his Christ.

It was beautiful.

I hope yours was, too.

Happy New Year!

Truly yours,

Jonathan

MANNY'S GYM
Four Seasons Drive
Toledo, Ohio

January 1

Hey, Rev,

Us Toledo Glassknees was backed up to our own five an I'm lookin at 95 yards of mud in the Crystal Bowl.

It's rainin four days. Water is standin in the field.

Boom! Boom! Two cracks an two yards. Third an eight. A obvious passin situation, right?

Wrong.

The quarter is over. We slosh alla way to the other end.

The manager comes out to the huddle an he cleans the mud outa my cleats an he says coach says I got the call.

The snap. *Wham!* Right through the middle. I cut back an I'm through the wall, tearin up field. Everybody's slidin. Nobody can catch me. I am in the end zone. We win, 6-O.

Wow! Do I feel good!

On the bus back, I'm thinkin I should oughta tell you about it because you can use it for a sermon illusionation.

You remember how the Lord told them guys if things don't go good in a town they should shake the dust offa their shoes an go somewheres else? Dust is dry mud, right? What I mean, it's like don't carry a grudge in your heart, see?

So at the start of the New Year, it's a new ball game. An if you're gonna get goin, you gotta clean out your cleats — cut the gook of the last year offa your shoes an travel clean an light for the next play.

I thought you could tell folks that if they wanna gain, they can't afford to have their cleats mucked up with last year's mud.

Your pal,

Hulk Hagarson

ARMIN LEGG, M.D.
Asthma Plaza
1998 Humerus Highway
Toledo, Ohio

January 2

Dear Mr. Versteeg,

No, at this point I cannot recommend your face for cosmetic surgery.

"Aging anxiety," let me assure you, is not uncommon at this time of New Year. May I suggest that a hopeful smile is all the lift you need.

I do notice, however, that you are sagging a bit at the other end, and maybe we should do something about that.

You and I are accustomed to seeing the New Year with two different faces, each standing for a different end of the year: the face of the infant New Year and the face of Old Father Time with his scythe — the baby and the blade, the birth and the burial. Our business as mortals is to wrest a blessing from both.

With the New Year are born new things: new opportunities, new challenges, new decisions — in fact, new life. There is your hope for a face-lift!

With the old year, old things have to die away and we have to learn to bury what is past. There is my hope for trimming your other end!

I can't think of a healthier prescription for starting the New Year than that fabled Chinese custom of canceling all past debts at New Year's Day — all debts: disappointments, hurt feelings, grudges, regrets! Why heap last year's burdens onto the baby New Year? A load like that would squash the little tyke. Do yourself a favor and leave them on the bent back of the Old Year.

Start your New Year like a baby — with a bright face and a bare behind!

Sincerely,

Armin Legg, M.D.

P.S. May we please have something on your account? You're a little behind.

Heart of the Forest
Black Mountain
North Carolina

January 4

Dear Bob,

I went out into the forest to watch the snow fall through the trees.

I stood a long while watching.

When at last I looked around me at the ground, I saw that the blowing snow had covered everything. Even the tracks I had made when I came out were covered with pure snow.

And I saw that, any way I went, ahead was covered with white.

I remembered Isaiah's promise: "though your sins be as scarlet, they shall be as white as snow."

Silently and gently God's mercy comes covering the sins of the past and giving us a clean new life.

Truly yours,

Jonathan

7 Camelot Circle
Toledo, Ohio

January 6

Dear Pastor Bob,

Last year when I went down to stand in line to give the license-plate people my money, instead of giving me new license plates for my car, they gave me a little sticker. They said I was supposed to stick it on my old license plate and pretend it was a new license plate.

This year I went down and gave them a sticker and told them they could stick it on the money I gave them last year and pretend it was new money.

They had a different suggestion about where I could stick it.

But what shall we think about sticking a lapel cross or a necklace cross on last year's same old person and pretending it's a new creation?

When Christ makes us new, he really changes us, doesn't he?

Simply sticking a little cross on the outside is not going to fool anyone, least of all God.

We have to let Christ change us into new people — his people. Don't get caught driving with expired plates!

Lovishly,

Guinevere Jones

RABBIT RUN VOLKSWAGON INC.
13 Upshaft Drive
Toledo, Ohio

January 8

Pastor Vorshtag:

I am regretful for the trouble you had. The reason you couldn't get the gearshift on your Rabbit to work is that the preheater hose connections had rusted off and allowed the hose to fall down and jam the linkage.

It is not uncommon. Let me explain.

Think of a church member who once was all steamed up, but got rusty and fell away. His linkage to the church no longer works, and what you have left is a shiftless Christian who is not geared in to the power train.

That is what happened to your automobile.

We can replace it or fix the old one.

It would be nice if you could save the old part.

'Wiedersehen!

Wolfgang von Krankcase
Service Manager

Limestone Collegiate Church
Fort Industry Square
Toledo, Ohio
January 10

Dear Brother Versteeg,

As one marathon man I know said after he was injured running and had to drop out of a race, "He who quits and limps away, lives to run another day."

Or as the writer of Ecclesiastes, who knew a thing or two about races, should have written: "There is a time to drop out, and there is a time to hang in."

The trick is to know which is which.

There's the Bullheaded-Bulldog Syndrome exemplified by King Pellinore in *Camelot* when he says, "When I sink my teeth into something, I sometimes have to leave them there."

And then there's the Faithful-unto-Death Syndrome exemplified by Sir Francis Drake when he prayed:

O Lord, when thou givest to thy servants to endeavor any great matter, grant us also to know that it is not the beginning, but the continuing of the same until it is thoroughly finished, which yieldeth the true glory; through Him that, for the finishing of thy work laid down his life, even Jesus Christ our Lord and Savior.

It all sheds light on St. Paul's boast in the Lord: "I have finished the race."

When we're on the wrong course — when we see the spiritual highway markers: "Wrong Way: Do Not Enter" —

it's time to turn around and get out. But when we're on the right course, we need to have grace and endurance to go all the way.

Fraternally,

I. Rant

Dictated by Dr. Rant but signed in his absence.

P.S. Sorry this letter is late. The Post Office returned it to us because the stamp fell off.

MANNY'S GYM
Four Seasons Drive
Toledo, Ohio

January 13

Hey, Rev,

Us Toledo Glassknees Semi-Pro football squad has got us a exhibition scrimmage against the Detroit Shock Absorbers which we are gonna play on Sunday after church.

We figure to get some of the spillover crowd from the Super Bowl. We are callin it the Punch Bowl.

Us human beans are so made that we gotta celebrate, an things like Bowl Games gives us a feelin of a Big Occasion. It makes life less daily an more significanter.

Me, I feel that way ever Sunday about celebratin the game of the Great Quarterback. For me, that makes ever Sunday Super Sunday.

On three!

Your pal,

Hulk Hagarson

362636 Starlet Drive
Hollywood, California

January 15

Dear V.,

Sorry to hear about the crimp the American automotive industry's slump is putting in economic conditions in your area, but I've got an idea which may help American manufacturers compete with foreign imports in gas economy by lowering the weight of their cars.

Leave off the brakes.

When was the last time you saw a motorist use his brakes?

Today brakes are obsolete. Remember the old Burma-Shave signs:

Big mistake
Some drivers make:
Rely on horn
Instead of brake.

Today it's a way of life. And death.

We don't use them: first clutch pedals, now brake pedals.

I don't have to remind you that we're rearing an entire generation (and I don't mean only the chronologically younger generation) — without brakes.

There are people who've thrown out all the restraints. "If it feels good, do it" — and never you mind whom you run down doing it, never mind how many smash-ups result.

Who needs brakes? The way to destruction is easy and broad.

Merrily,

Gloria Glitz

BUCKHOISTER INVESTMENTS
One at Wall
New York, N. Y.

18 January

Dear Client:

Back in the days when one of America's Big Three automakers was touting its biggest cars with tv ads featuring the famous Latin American movie star Retardo Mentalblock, had that automaker instead been studying and learning from Japanese auto makers, that automaker might have been leading the U.S. industry all along instead of teetering on the brink of bye-bye until it was rescued by government bail-out.

This raises a spiritual point made a long time ago by Karl Barth: What model of human being will survive at this point in history? The old model won't make it in contemporary conditions.

The old luxury-model human being, you remember, came equipped with heavy warfare, wasteful economy, exploitation of have-nots, and eight-cylinder selfishness. The Maker is recalling that model.

How do we shape up to survive in coming years? There's a new design.

It's time to re-tool!

Yours for better investments,

Louis Buckhoister
Financial Consultant

1776 American Way
Toledo, Ohio

January l0

Dear Revrund Dursteen,

The reason I don't come to your church is that it has got too many hypocrites in it.

You people are not one-hundred-and-ten-percent Americans. I can tell that just by looking at the parking lot.

Let's start with you. You yourself, Revrund Dursteen, are driving a Volkswagen (when it drives, that is, and serves you right when it don't.) Never mind telling me it was built in Pennsylvania — that's just infiltration by the fifth colyum. What about the welfare of Detroit and our beloved city of Toledo? Imports is un-American.

Real Americans buy American — like for example a Opel from Buick, a Alliance from AMC, a Colt from Chrysler, or one of them nice little Ford Fiestas.

Just wait till we get them foreign import quotas on, and then you'll see what American know-how and free enterprise and good old competition can do to restore the American automobile market in spite of hypocrites like yourself.

And that's the reason why I don't come to your church, because you don't do nothing about hypocrisy.

Loyally yours,

Claude A. Merkin

GUMBO GATE MOTEL
5251 Beaucaire
New Orleans, Louisiana

January 21

Hey, Rev,

I bet you're sorry now you didn't come to the Super Bowl with us. Whatcha gonna do next summer that you're savin your vacation for that can be half as good as a Super Bowl? Specially seein how much you like football.

I got us seats on the 45. Butch an me is gonna wear our Toledo Glassknees jackets, so look for us on tv. We'll be easy to spot — I'll wave.

I been hearin everbody say Super Bowl is our national religion, so I been comparin it with the worship of the Roman Emperor you was tellin us about in Bible times, you know?

They usta say Cowboy Movies was a kinda religion about the frontier. Now they say football is supposed to be a religion about modren America.

There's the goalposts everbody bows down to an tries to get to, an there's teamwork an there's individuality, an you gotta be fast an hard an tough, an you fight to win. There's the cheerleaders an the money an the ceremony an the crowd yellin and the bands an everthing. At leastways, that's what folks wanna believe.

But that's not the way it really is. I'm not just talkin about how there's holdin on every play. I mean, nobody really lives a football game, so how can it be our national religion?

But then, how many folks you know really live Christianity?

I made us a John 3:16 banner.

Wisht you was here.

Your pal,

Hulk Hagarson

ATTILA D. HUNN, D.D.S.
Canal Route #3
Toledo, Ohio

January 23

Dear Mr. Versteeg,

We have now taken impressions of your mouth three times and we have now cast the plate for your partial three times. Each time the partial has fit the mold of your teeth perfectly, but when you come into the office for a fitting, the partial will not fit your teeth — not with any amount of wiggling and wobbling, pinching and pushing and prying.

After three tries, we are forced to conclude that the problem is your mouth.

Your mouth keeps changing. You would need a rubber partial.

Unless you can find some way to control your mouth, we cannot solve your problem.

There's a parable there.

Sincerely,

Attila D. Hunn, D.D.S.

P.S. May we please have something on your account?

666 Shoehorn Manor
Toledo, Ohio

29 January

Ding-a-ling:

Knock off the chimes or take my name off the roll.
I will not be a member of a church that keeps waking me
up.

Instantly,

Henrietta Peckingham

WOLFGANG VON KRANKASE

RABBIT RUN VOLKSWAGON INC.
13 Upshaft Drive
Toledo, Ohio

February 1

Pastor Vorshtag:

I am regretful that your attitude toward your Rabbit is so negative.

Your problem is that you do not look on the bright side of things.

When you closed your door and the window fell out, you acted as if it were some kind of calamity.

Think of it as air conditioning.

When the bumper rusted, you acted as if there were something wrong with our paint.

Think of it as texture.

Now that a spring has been squeaking, you act as if it were a nuisance.

Think of it as chirping.

The silver lining, Pastor Vorshtag: look for the silver lining.

The bill for oiling your chirp is $14.78.

'Wiedersehen!

Wolfgang von Krankcase
Service Manager

362636 Starlet Drive
Hollywood, California

February 4

Dear V.,

Today in dance class our teacher read to us:

In a modern world it takes effort even to be receptive — to break the momentum of daily compulsions long enough to receive impressions.*

It's true. Daily compulsions prevent us from receiving daily bread from the Lord.

All those things we've got to do, all those places we've got to go, all those people we've got to see — no wonder we forget to wait quietly before the Lord.

When we do get to the Lord, it's with our own daily compulsions. That's why in prayer we're compulsive talkers.

We forget the better prayer of being quiet, open to receive the Spirit.

Part of it is defensiveness. So many people — and TV sets and radios — are bombarding us with daily compulsions of their own, that we develop a protective shell so nothing can penetrate and get to us.

"Ask and ye shall receive"? How can we hope to receive unless we come to a resting position, put forth the braking effort to break the momentum of our daily compulsions?

Luv a Bunch?

Gloria Glitz

---

*Miriam Winslow, *Dance: A Basic Educational Technique,* Frederick Rand Rogers, Editor, Dance Horizons, New York, 1980, p. 81.

Heart of the Forest
Black Mountain
North Carolina

February 6

Dear Bob,

No, I don't find winter in the woods down here confining; liberating, rather.

I am often outside walking and caring for the animals. My exercise is splitting firewood.

Brother Fire cooks my food and keeps me warm and lends me light for reading.

This winter I have read Thomas Mann's *Magic Mountain* and *Joseph and His Brothers.* I have read *Anna Karenina, The Tempest,* and *MacBeth; The Wasteland,* Poe's poetry, Plato's *Crito,* Forster's *Passage to India,* and Shaw's *Back to Methuselah.*

I have read some of Browning's poetry, and much of Keats's; Hazlitt's essays; and Conrad's short stories. I have re-read the gospels — they are brief reading — and marveled again at the Figure who could have inspired in those writers such faith.

So you see my winters free me to soar in delight.

Do you think life here in the forest is primitive, not having electricity and television?

Truly yours,

Jonathan

7 Camelot Circle
Toledo, Ohio

February 8

Dear Pastor Bob,

My friend Sylvia was terribly down the other day. And then she got further down because she thought it was sinful to get down.

That could go on forever.

Someone had told her that a Christian should never feel blue — it was some kind of lack of faith.

As if Christians never needed a faith lift!

I remembered that talk you and I had about the difference between real joy and mere five-and-ten-cent-store giddiness. (Whatever happened to five-and-ten-cent stores, anyway?)

I tried to explain to Sylvia that none of the great figures of the Old Testament and none of the disciples was ever depicted as living a care-free life. I told her how the writers of the Bible identified Jesus himself with the "man of sorrows and acquainted with grief."

And then that beautiful hymn began to sing in my heart and I shared it with her:

O Joy that seekest me through pain,
I cannot close my heart to thee;
I trace the rainbow through the rain,
And feel the promise is not vain
That morn shall tearless be.

If you look to the sun through your tears, you see rainbows.

Maybe joy is what helps us to be faithful in sadness. Or maybe that's the way joy comes.

What do you think?

Lovishly,

Guinevere Jones

Limestone Collegiate Church
Fort Industry Square
Toledo, Ohio

February 11

Dear Brother Versteeg,

I'm glad you enjoy the sight of youngsters skating and playing hockey on the river ice. Thus you see that when the world confronts us with a frozen condition, we might well find some way to turn the world's hardness to our advantage — to go skating on our way.

Unfortunate, on the other hand, about your frozen parsonage pipes. As I tell my congregation (broadcast time is twelve noon), when the waters of compassion freeze up within our souls, we are no longer useful to the Lord. And if the freeze is hard enough, it can burst and ruin our spiritual system altogether.

The moral being, that to overcome the frozen outside of us is challenging; whereas to be frozen within is chilling indeed.

I remind you that when Dante reached the very center of hell he found there the devil frozen immobile in ice. Dante climbed over the icy monster and began his ascent to Paradise.

Yours for the Gospel glow,

I. Rant

Dictated by Dr. Rant, but signed in his absence.

362636 Starlet Drive
Hollywood, California

February 13

Dear V.,

Friend of mine gave me a big lift today.

I was feeling low — been making the rounds, knocking on doors, getting turned down.

I know it's a tough business. Sometimes it seems nothing you do makes any difference. Banging your head against the stone wall.

Then I saw my friend and told her about it. She agreed that sometimes all our efforts don't make a dent.

That's all. We went our ways.

Then it dawned on me what a difference she had made in my day by caring enough to listen to me and understand and not tell me I shouldn't feel that way.

We can get results: we can do things for others, and it does make a difference.

Praise the Lord!

Luv a Bunch!

Gloria Glitz

7 Camelot Circle
Toledo, Ohio

February 15

Dear Pastor Bob,

A friend who has a farm a mile outside the city came in with a snow plow on his tractor and pushed the snow out of the alley where I park my car behind the house.

It was really a nice thing for him to do. That was a lot of snow.

Unfortunately, all the snow he pushed away from my garage got piled up in front of my neighbor's garage.

It took my neighbor two days with a hand shovel to dig out. He was not pleased.

I'm afraid that's the way it's going to be in our society with the new trends — we'll clear all our problems away and dump them on our neighbors, the poor.

Lovishly but concerned,

Guinevere Jones

Heart of the Forest
Black Mountain
North Carolina

February 18

Dear Bob,

I was interested to hear about those ice fishermen — the
ones who had to be rescued off the ice drifting in Lake Erie.

I was especially interested that some of them are repeat-
ers who now blame the Coast Guard who rescued them!

I remember the rhyme my father used to love to play
with, and I've adapted it:

Just how slow
Would an ice floe flow
If an ice floe did flow slow?
It would flow as slow
As an ice floe flowed
If an ice floe did flow slow.

Out on the seeming-solid ice, pursuing each his own
pleasure, lost each in his own purposes and preoccupations,
heedless alike of warming and warning, and then suddenly
dangerously adrift on the deceptive and disintegrating ice
broken off from the mainland — even so do we on the sea of
life get lost from God.

We are ignorant of our fatal separation until it is too late,
and we would blame our predicament on those who would
save us.

Who will save us?

Truly yours,

Jonathan

1812 Foundry Lane
Toledo, Ohio

January 26

Dear Reverend Vernstein,

I enclose a check for the full amount of the new carillon I am donating to your church as a memorial to my late husband, Herbert.

Herbert loved the sound of bells. *The Hunchback of Notre Dame* was his favorite movie.

It was Herbert's love of bells that sent him into the business of manufacturing door chimes, having heard opportunity, well, ring, so to speak.

And although the business kept him too busy ever to attend church himself, Herbert always had a moment to pause outside and listen to church bells ringing.

And upon hearing a church carillon, Herbert would always remark how the bells rang out reminders of promise, of hope, even of wistfulness.

I will take great comfort in knowing that each time our carillon plays, it plays for Herbert.

Sorrowfully,

Mrs. Herbert Peal

WINTER WONDERLAND LODGE
12 Ski Lift Way
Lake Placid, New York

February 23

Hey, Rev,

Gettin this job with the snow crew has worked out just like I figured: I ain't payin to see the Winter Olympics; they're payin me.

What I like best is the ski jump.

This guy comes outta this chute, see. He comes skiin down as fast as he can go. He gets to the curved-up end. He straightens up an he shoots off the edge right out into space flyin — great!

Nothin your eye can see holds him up. Truth is he's sailin through the air because he's surrounded by wind.

Faith — I figure faith is like that. When you're goin downhill an you think you've come to the end, you straighten up an throw yourself on the invisible Spirit of the Lord, an that'll carry you a long ways.

Ony He don't let you down.

Your pal,

Hulk Hagarson

362636 Starlet Drive
Hollywood, California

February 20

Dear V.,

Remember the play we used to do about the man whose arms and legs got amputated — was it Peter Handke's *Clown Play?*

Everytime he lost another part of his body, someone would say to him, "You know how it is, Mr. Smith: you can't have everything."

I've got friends who feel like that in life: feel that they keep getting cut up and losing, until they can't cope with life anymore.

That's when I treasure Philippians 4:13: "I can do all things through Christ which strengtheneth me."

Maybe I can't do everything, but all the things I have to do.

I am God's child, and I can cope with life and the world. He has created me with the power to respond to life's challenges creatively.

I am an effectively functioning adult with some outstanding qualities. I have my limitations, but I also have my excellences.

That's the way God made me. I can cope.

Luv a Bunch!

Gloria Glitz

Heart of the Forest
Black Mountain
North Carolina

February 27

Dear Bob,

This morning I went to visit my friend who lives in
town. I decided to walk on my hands. People on the street
stared at me.

But I think that every now and then we all need to do
some hand-balancing. We need to stand on our heads and let
gravity pull the other way. Whether or not it's good for our
circulation, it's necessary for our spiritual equilibrium.

It's one of the first rules of creative thinking: What
would happen if I turned it upside down?

God turns things upside down, too. That's the way he
keeps the world going.

Is evil on top and good crushed down? "...(T)he way of
the wicked He turneth upside down."

G. K. Chesterton said that the difference between a mere
rebel and a truly revolutionary thinker was this: the mere rebel only wants the wheel to turn half way, so he can come
out on top and stay on top. The truly revolutionary thinker,
on the other hand, keeps on turning things all the way over
in his mind, and keeps the wheels of progress rolling
forward.

In this sense, Jesus is a profoundly revolutionary person
(read the Magnificat!): He keeps upsetting men's smug ar-
rangements.

The Cross is the lever, Calvary the fulcrum, with which
Jesus overturns our worldly values — our definitions of success — and overthrows Satan's temptations.

Bottoms up!

Truly yours,

Jonathan

ATTILA D. HUNN, D.D.S.
Canal Route #3
Toledo, Ohio

March 2

Dear Mr. Versteeg,

I am naturally pleased that you are happy with your new partial denture, or, as you put it, that I "restoreth your teeth."

However, perhaps there are a few points we didn't cover sufficiently in our brochure and talks.

First, it really is not considered good form for you to stop and grin at your reflection in every mirror you pass. People are talking.

And it really is not necessary for you to plop your plate into the water glass at dinner. Cleanliness is not all that close to godliness.

You should leave your denture in place when you eat. Its purpose is not only cosmetic, but practical.

Getting your teeth restored ought to be like getting your soul restored. It's not just so you can look good. There ought to be some bite in it.

Sincerely,

Attila D. Hunn, D.D.S.

P.S. May we please have something on your account?

SPRING

SPRING TRAINING AND WATERPROOF CHRISTIANS

362636 Starlet Drive
Hollywood, California

March 5

Dear V.,

No, I've never seen *Beauty and the Beast* on stage, but the marvelous Cocteau film is one of my all time favorites.

If the moral is that the love of Beauty can transform a beast into a right handsome prince, it fits in well with our current attempts to kiss frogs into royal personages, to listen the lost into loveliness, and to love-bomb the dead to life.

Truth is, though, that the illusion of beauty (it's in the eye of the beholder) has turned some princely people into beasts.

As the Ubangi said, it has to do with cultural conditioning. We Christians, however, are called to be conditioned by the Cross.

The prophet warned us that Christ would surprise us:

. . . he hath no form nor comeliness; and when we shall see him, there is no beauty that we should desire him.

Yet Christ is still our hope to transform all our beastliness into the beauty of love.

"Let the beauty of Jesus be seen in me!"

Luv a Bunch!

Gloria Glitz

Heart of the Forest
Black Mountain
North Carolina

March 8

Dear Bob,

I thought about you this morning while I was taking
some exercise along my second favorite path through the
forest and, within a hundred yards, I startled nine rabbits,
each of which darted away into the trees.

I wished you could have been here to see that there really are rabbits that run.

I'm sorry to hear that you have now had to buy your
Volkswagen's fourth alternator at $107.00 each, and sorry
to hear that your ace greasemonkey Wolfgang von Krankcase
has no idea at all what burns out your alternator every
fifteen thousand miles.

Perhaps you should be philosophical and consider that
maybe Someone is trying to get something through to you.

Lately have you read Psalm 20:7 — "Some trust in chariots, and some in horses: but we will remember the name of
the Lord our God"? Or Isaiah 31:1 — "Woe to them that. . .
trust in chariots. . . "

Are there alternators in chariots? Or am I swinging low?

Truly yours,

Jonathan

Limestone Collegiate Church
Fort Industry Square
Toledo, Ohio

March 11

Dear Brother Versteeg,

Yes, I, too, was delighted when the Pope came to visit our country.

But I'm afraid you're in danger of overlooking the greatest benefit of his visit.

You see, the Pope stands for something — and Someone. The Pope is an ambassador for Christ, as we all should be.

Not everyone will agree with some of the things the Pope stands for, but maybe we all ought to applaud the fact that he does stand for something and Someone.

The great benefit for us, therefore, would be if the Pope's positive stands were to inspire us, too, to define where it is that we stand.

Any fool can be negative. Don't tell me what you're "agin;" tell me what you're for. That takes some guts.

Furthermore, the Pope has had the courage to stand for his principles in the teeth of dangerous opposition and at the risk of unpopularity. He has taken his stand when it has cost him.

Protestants who trace their lineage to Martin Luther should be heartened by the presence in our day of another man who dares to say, "Here I stand."

The New Testament calls all ambassadors for Christ to take their stand for Christ who stands for — and stands with — us. It calls us to take our stand for Christ's cause.

The Pope is an inspiration.
Anyway, that's where I stand.
How about you?

Sincerely,

I. Rant

Dictated by Dr. Rant, but signed in his absence.

7 Camelot Circle
Toledo, Ohio

March 15

Dear Pastor Bob,

Last night I asserted myself.

After dinner I did the dishes, started the laundry, bathed the children, and was putting them to bed when my husband, who was watching a tv movie "without commercial interruptions," asked me to bring him a plate of snacks. I told him to get his own.

I'm going to put some interruptions back into my life.

I'm going to interrupt my life so I can take time out:

— to read
— to meditate
— to go to the john
— to play with my children.

I'm going to interrupt what has become the commercial part of my life so I can take time out to live the real part of my life.

In the margin of Ecclesiastes I've written, "To every plug there is a time to pull."

Lovishly,

Guinevere Jones

MANNY'S GYM
Four Seasons Drive
Toledo, Ohio

March 16

Hey, Rev,

At the Winter Olympics I seen a lot of accomplishment, an I thought you could use some advice.

It's simple.

Olympic athletes have a goal, an they work toward it every day.

Same way, we all gotta decide what our goal is — I mean, the kinda folks we wanna be for the Lord — an work toward it, "press forward" every day.

I like 1 Corinthians 9:24-27.

Your pal,

Hulk Hagarson

JONATHAN WOODMAN

Heart of the Forest
Black Mountain
North Carolina

March 19

Dear Bob,

This week we had a woodland tragedy.

An old tree, that had been here much longer than anyone can remember, her roots like gnarled fingers clutching the earth, was torn loose in a windstorm, and when she fell she crushed one of our little squirrel creatures.

We all sorrowed, but we were not angry. That same force of gravity which had made the little squirrel creature's life possible — bringing spring water down the mountains to the streams, holding the little squirrel creature close to its mother on the earth, allowing the little squirrel creature to run and jump through the trees — also made the tree fall.

Somehow it must all be within the providence of God.

This week also I went into town to sell wood and buy provisions. Young men laughed at my long hair and my clothes and they called me nasty names. I cannot understand their unkindness. How are they part of the providence of God?

Thank you for your answer.

Truly Yours,

Jonathan

FALN-BY-THE-WAYSIDE
99 River Road
Toledo, Ohio

March 22

Reverend Sir:

I want you to know that you have thoroughly upset me by removing my name from the church rolls.

It's true that I haven't attended or contributed for three years, and it's true that I just didn't have time to respond to your calls and letters.

But, in my opinion, I'm worshipping God just as truly on the golf course as a bunch of you hypocrites are inside a building.

Church membership should be a spiritual thing; you make it one inconvenience after another — always wanting me to be here or there, wanting me to do this or that, and always wanting me to give, give, give!

Now I'm going to have to go to the inconvenience of finding another church to belong to. Somebody's always asking me to go to church. I used to be able to say, "I belong to the Church of the Warm Heart," and that got me off the hook.

So I say this is just the inconvenience to crown all the other inconveniences you've been to me, and I think it's pretty highhanded of you — very unChristlike!

Summarily,

A. Strayer

362636 Starlet Drive
Hollywood, California

March 25

Dear V.,

'Went the other night to see Marcel Marceau.
Wow!
Movement, gesture, posture — he speaks a beautiful universal language of mime.
Don't get me wrong. I love beautiful and significant words.
But I love beautiful and significant movement, too.
The way I read my T.N.T., Jesus, who could put together some *muy** powerful words, also had an eye for the powerful action.
He praised the woman who silently anointed him for burial. He warned us that not everyone who said, "Lord! Lord!" was making it, but rather the person who did the will of his Father. And he himself dumbly performed his passion to show us the love of God.
Ray Birdwhistell says that the average person speaks words for a total of only ten or eleven minutes per day (except preachers, I guess), but I think, as far as the Lord's concerned we're putting across a message all the rest of the time, too.
Actions speak.

Luv a Bunch!

Gloria Glitz

---

*(Just in case you don't speak Spanish, V.,the word means "very.")

West Ohio Conference
471 E. Broad St. Suite P
Columbus, Ohio

28 March

My Dear Brother Versteeg:

Let me remind you that according to some the season of Lent was originally named from the Latin word meaning "slow," as in the musical direction, *lento.*

Ah, bitter irony!

In our society, the modern pastor finds that he must play the Lenten season *presto,* at the very least, and, more probably, *prestissimo.* (If you still know as little Latin and music as you did when you were in seminary, I should translate: fast and fastest.)

Like a conductor whose metronome is on fast-forward, today's manic pastor flails his way through the holy score of Lent, hurling leaves of music hither and yon, turning dirge into ditty.

He races through Lent to finish in a breathless blaze of Easter glory before he knows it. He himself scarcely has time to repent before it's over.

That's the way life is.

Our Lenten rubric should be: *Festina lente* — make haste slowly.

Take time to go slowly, Brother Versteeg; take time. Invest a little time in eternity.

Advisedly,

Bishop Bright Roader

666 Shoehorn Manor
Toledo, Ohio

3 April

Versteeg:

I tried all day Monday to reach you because I heard about
that sermon of yours and I intend to set you straight.

I finally got the church secretary and checked on your
whereabouts.

Turns out, at 8:30 you were at a breakfast meeting at the
hospital with the other clergymen, supposedly discussing ways
to provide better patient care. A free breakfast, that's what it
was.

The rest of the morning you were locked away in your
study working on a worship service for the District Missions
Convocation. Why plan worship? Why can't it be spon-
taneous?

In the afternoon, you were off worrying about the Ecumenical Communications Commission. What business have you
got wasting time on our city's television ministry? After all,
our church doesn't broadcast.

At night you actually found a few minutes to counsel with
an individual before you prepared for and went to the Ad-
ministrative Board meeting.

All this time, I was trying to reach you, and by now I've
forgotten what it was I needed to straighten you out about.

But I want to advise you to stick to your business and stay
in your office. Your parishioners pay your salary, and they
expect you to be available.

I tell you this for your own good.

Helpfully,

Henrietta Peckingham

7 Camelot Circle
Toledo, Ohio

April 5

Dear Pastor Bob,

My best friend starts a letter:

> The boys (aged ten months and three years) and I
> went to church this a.m. thru pouring rain. If you have
> an inventor acquaintance (because of you my friend
> thinks I've got all these weird friends), he could make a
> mint from an umbrella to be used while carrying two
> children, a purse, and a diaper bag!

One of those mornings I wonder if it's worth it, then decide it
is, once I get there!

My friend is Episcopalian. I always wondered why the Lord
didn't waterproof more Methodists. No wonder you don't dare
more than dab 'em when you baptize 'em!

Reminds me of the guy who told his gal he loved her so
much he'd go through fire for her, climb the highest mountain
for her, swim the deepest ocean for her, and he'd be over to see
her Saturday if it didn't rain.

I'll bet when the Hebrew children made their miraculous
crossing of the sea that opened before them, the first ones
through got their toes wet.

Gotta run. Gonna re-read Galatians and see if Paul's list of
the armor of the Spirit includes umbrellas and galoshes.

Lovishly,

Guinevere Jones

MANNY'S GYM
Four Seasons Drive
Toledo, Ohio

April 8

Hey, Rev,

I been thinkin we oughta break us a World Record an
get ourselves into that Guiness Book.
Last Sunday's comix named three world records:
— most parking tickets
— world record sermon
— most boxing matches.
Which one you wanna go for?
We already got too many people ain't doin nothin in
church but parkin.
But if you go for the world's longest sermon, you pro-
bly gonna take care of the parkin problem an end up with
the world's smallest congregation.
So that leaves the record for "the greatest recorded
number of fights in a career."
Seems like us modren-day Christians today don't read
what St. Paul wrote about fightin the good fight an jabbin
the air. We think Christians oughta stay outta fights.
Closest we come is some easy shadow boxin to show off.
These days, when the Lord goes in to clean out the temple,
we don't even root for him.
We gotta care enough about our Main Event that we're
willin to take on some principalities an powers, go to the
mat for justice and righteousness' sake.
Ain't the Devil still walkin aroun needin to get popped
on the snout? I mean, is the Devil shakin hands, or is he
comin out punchin low?

So I say let's start workin on the career fights record.

Maybe, better than the Guiness, we'll make the Book of Life.

You in my corner?

Your pal,

Hulk Hagarson

666 Shoehorn Manor
Toledo, Ohio

11 April

Versteeg:

I just phoned the church office to complain about the way
my last copy of the newsletter was crumpled when it got to my
house, and the secretary told me you were home trying to
think of something to write for this week's newsletter.

I thought to myself, "Oh, no! Here comes that inevitable
non-letter about not being able to write a letter" — always a
disgustingly coy cop-out.

Well, I'm not going to let you get away with it.

Don't you give me that self-pitying "Lenten burn-out"
routine.

If you would work harder and spend less time dashing
about, spend more time filling your mind with worthwhile
thoughts, you would have an uplifting message for your
parish.

Read your Bible — boy, do I wish you'd read your Bible!
You'd find out that the prophets were all busy men living in
pressure-packed situations. And they delivered.

God works in busy times, Versteeg.

Hop to it!

Forthrightly,

Henrietta Peckingham

362636 Starlet Drive
Hollywood, California

April 14

Dear V.,

No is not a dirty word.

'Other night I went to see the road company of what used to be my favorite performing group, Second City.

Some of what went on was like the adolescent urge to scribble "dirty" words on walls.

It was as if we'd gotten together to thumb our noses at — or the more mod equivalent, to "moon" — all of society's no-no's.

Next day I read Ellen Goodman's article about how, if some unliberated males had their way, the modern woman would no longer feel free to say "No" when she felt like saying "No."

You once told me that Karl Barth, astounded by the thoughts being published by his fellow theologians, rushed into print with a book of his own entitled *"Nein!"*

I remember, too, that that classic of nay-saying, The Ten Commandments, was heavy into *"Nein!"* and *"Verboten!"*

And while I believe that our Lord's impulse to put things positively — "You shall love the Lord and your neighbor" — was right as rain, he was also able to say, "Do not be as the hypocrites are," and other great "No"s. Check it out.

How can we say "Yes" to life unless we say "No" to suicide? How can we say "Yes" to health unless we say "No" to dissipation? How can we say "Yes" to freedom unless we say "No" to slavery?

No way.

Luv a Bunch!

Gloria Glitz

Heart of the Forest
Black Mountain
North Carolina

April 17

Dear Bob,

When I came home tonight, I found in front of my
threshold a small pool of blood.

Strange how you can recognize blood, even in the semi-
darkness.

No animal's cut foot — there were no tracks, there was
no other blood nearby. No bird from a tree, not that I could
tell.

Had someone come here in the forest to my door hurt?
Or cut himself here?

I worried for whomever it was that bled. I wished I had
been here to help.

I searched the forest. I called out. No one. No other sign.

What an urgent cry blood is!

Whose blood was it?

Truly yours,

Jonathan

666 Shoehorn Manor
Toledo, Ohio

April 18

Versteeg:

Don't you get huffy with me about missing your Good Friday service! Friday is my bowling night.

Combine it with Easter.

I heard about a church where, when people came in on Easter morning, there was a coffin and everything was somber like a funeral and the message was, "Jesus is dead."

Then they opened the lid of the casket and a bunch of helium-filled balloons flew out and everybody began to celebrate because Jesus had arisen.

Why can't you think of something creative and dramatic like that?

Then maybe more people would come to your Good Friday services — not to mention the others.

But don't do it just to please me; I'm not coming to that church until they get rid of you.

Forthrightly,

Henrietta Peckingham

P.S. I'll bet the plays you write and direct are dull, too.

Limestone Collegiate Church
Fort Industry Square
Toledo, Ohio

April 21

Dear Brother Versteeg,

In Holy Week God takes the worst and transforms it into the best.

The Holy Spirit renews our minds and we are transformed, our lives made new.

I see it happening to people all the time. It happens for me. I know it is true.

"Behold, I make all things new!"

It is God's Easter gift.

Happy Easter!

I. Rant

Dictated by Dr. Rant, but signed in his absence.

362636 Starlet Drive
Hollywood, California

April 22

Dear V.,

In *Pirates of Penzance* I've got a friend who knows an usher who slipped me in to see the show — super!

Ever since, Sir Arthur Sullivan's maniacal music has been zipping around in my brain. Only sometimes, like a drifting radio signal, ghost strains of Arthur Sullivan's *Onward Christian Soldiers!* intermingle with the *Pirate* sounds.

And that got me to thinking about *The Lost Chord* — which I haven't heard since I was a kid. I used to think it was The Neatest Song!

Now that I'm older, of course, I know that (at least on the scales we've got) we know all the chords there are. What made that chord Sir Arthur struck and which then struck him — the chord that left the soul of the organ and entered into his soul — so special had to be where it came in the musical progression.

It's that way with the great note of Easter joy, isn't it? You have to hear the Easter chord in its context — "was crucified, dead, and buried." Then the Easter chord — "on the third day He rose again" — enters your soul with all the thrill of its resolving, surprising joy.

Luv a Bunch!

Gloria Glitz

MANNY'S GYM
Four Seasons Drive
Toledo, Ohio

April 28

Hey, Rev,

I kin always count on three things to tell me it's spring
— the crocus, the robin, an the crack of the bat.

Maybe you think that the threat of a pro players' strike
don't infect semipros like us Toledo Glassknees, but that is
where you are wrong.

When the big leaguers are playin, fan enthusiasm
builds up for the whole sport.

Like Easter. When we remember how the Big Leaguer
played His game of life, we can get all excited about our
own games of life.

Happy Easter and happy Spring Trainin!

Your Pal,

Hulk Hagarson

THE GOLDEN ARCHES
5 Billion Bolted Downs
McDonaldland, N. C.

May 3

Dear Coach,

I've decided to take the job in Toledo. I hope I won't be an embarrassment to you.

I know that when I was studying acting with you (or, as you used to put it, when we were learning about acting together), you were heavy into Shaw and Shakespeare and urged us to study them. You know how much acting Shaw and Shakespeare in America pays? But selling hamburgers — wow!

You know how many Americans know Candida from Coriolanus? But the role I play is the most instantly recognized character in America today. What John Lennon said years ago of the Beatles is true of my character today: "better known than Jesus."

Besides, it's a chance to do a lot of good.

You remember doing bike-safety shows with me in schools. Now we also have a program of providing places for parents to stay while their children are in the hospital. Maybe I can get one of those started there in Toledo.

I guess my point is pretty trite, but important anyway: a person should be glad to be able to find ways to use his job to help his fellow man.

And at the worst, hamburgers in moderation probably won't kill you.

Oh, yes; I'm bringing Hamburglar with me.

See ya, Prof!

Ronald

PARKSIDE MEADOWS
St. Charles, Missouri

May 8

Dear Bob,

Do not be a hypocrite on Mother's Day.

Do not send pretty pictures to Mother while you pollute the environment until it is unfit for her baby.

Do not send candy to Mother while you pursue economic policies which force her baby to starve.

Do not send flowers to Mother while you poison the air her baby breathes.

Do not send cards to Mother while you print the draft-registration cards and militaristic menus which will napalm her babies.

Happy Mother's Day!

Mom

Heart of the Forest
Black Mountain
North Carolina

May 14

Dear Bob,

I walk through my forest and I look at my friends the trees. I worry about them.

A nuclear war would kill them, and they are innocent.

Humans aren't. Forgiven, yes; innocent, no.

Developers are already destroying the rain forests of the Amazon. One-third of the oxygen in the United States is generated by the Amazon rain forests.

Maybe it doesn't matter: after a nuclear war, there'd be no one left to breathe the oxygen.

Let's persuade the politicians to scrap the bombs and plant trees.

Yours for life,

Jonathan Woodman

362636 Starlet Drive
Hollywood, California

May 21

Dear V.,
   I just finished shooting a new commercial.
   I carry a giant box of detergent, twenty-two feet tall.
Of course it's an optic, but it looks great.
   The pitch is: "The detergent for big cleaning jobs."
Cute, huh?
   It made me think about Jesus who washes away the
sins of the whole world. He's the detergent of my soul.
   I'm talking to a friend of mine who writes songs, and
maybe we're going to do something with the idea. It'll be
my first disc. Cute, huh?

                        Luv a Bunch!

                        Gloria Glitz

44 Conceit Circle
Toledo, Ohio

May 24

Dear Rev. Bob,

When I was a child, my mother taught me that it was vulgar to say "Gee!" or "Gee whiz!" because the word *Gee* was, as the dictionary says, "a euphemism for *Jesus.*"

(Imagine: a euphemism for "Jesus," the sweetest name! Nowadays, if you say "Gee," some nerve-twitch moron says, "No; GTE.")

But, as any old-time farmer can tell you, "Gee!" also means to tell a mule to go to the right, or simply to move faster, as in *giddyap!*

The reason for all this farmyard philology is that I was wondering whether we might hop on the T-shirt bandwagon with G-shirts, G in this instance standing for God, or God's Person, and reminding us in our mulish moments that it is time for us to get going and going right for God's sake.

Still got your silkscreen?

Whimsically yours,

John Dunn

Limestone Collegiate Church
Fort Industry Square
Toledo, Ohio

May 29

Dear Brother Versteeg,

Since you ask my advice about your church sign, I have fitted into my already crowded schedule time to send these thoughts about your problem.

As I understand it, your first complaint is that your church's front-lawn sign can't be read until one is past it, and you're wondering if it would be possible to (1) put an additional sign down on the corner, (2) relocate the present sign, or (3) turn the sign around.

Have you thought instead about turning your church around? That might make folks take notice.

What about God's sign? When he wanted people to notice his love, he put a Cross up on a hill. Of course, that's pretty radical, and I doubt you'll go for it.

And your second problem with signs is that your denominational markers are faded out, eh? I suggest you leave them that way. They're telling the turth, and I'm for a little truth in advertising when it comes to religion. If anybody's denominationalism is faded, Brother Versteeg, it's yours.

Or, if you insist on getting new markers, then I suggest you renew your denominational loyalty as well — I notice you were absent from last Friday's District Seminar on the Treatment of Desk-Top Stapler Wounds.

Here at my own parish, I'm suggesting to the Board of Trustees that we put up a new church sign reading:

RESTAURANT. Everyone in this town goes to restaurants. After all, I am serving soul food.

How's that for food for thought?

Fraternally,

I. Rant

Dictated by Dr. Rant, but signed in his absence.

REV. I. RANT

SUMMER

DOG DAYS AND DISCIPLESHIP

362636 Starlet Drive
Hollywood, California

June 3

Dear V.,

So you're going to preach about *The Serpent!*

You know, when I was a kid, instead of "the serpent was more subtil than any beast of the field," I thought it said, "the serpent was more *supple* than any beast of the field."

It was a natural mistake, right? After all, the serpent is more supple than any beast of the field.

Today we teach flexibility as a grace, and in some ways it is — especially when it comes to not insisting on one's own way or to being able to fit oneself to changing needs.

But other times the Tempter tries to persuade us that it is never right to be inflexible, tries to persuade us that even the stone tablets of the Commandments can be bent without breaking.

Think of all those respectable citizens the Nazis persuaded to be flexible enough to make room for Dachau. Think of the ways we ourselves twist our standards or bend the law under the feather-weight of personal advantage or even simply convenience.

I know the Serpent, and he really is supple.

Bend a leg!

Gloria Glitz

MANNY'S GYM
Four Seasons Drive
Toledo, Ohio

June 7

Hey, Rev,

Lotsa Spanish-speaking ballplayers aroun nowdays provin that ol Spanish folksong:

You don't gotta know the lingo
If you just wanna strike 'em out!

They got themselves agents who teach 'em to talk American an the first words they say is, "Hey, Gringo, renegotiate el contracto."

I was thinkin how many folks talk a good game when it comes to being Christian. They know the religious lingo, all the whoop an holler, all the pious slogans, an all the glib phrases.

But the Big Coach taught us that what counts is what kinda stuff you put on the ball — feedin the hungry, clothin the naked, visitin the prisoners.

Not how ya say the Name,
But how ya play the game —

that's what counts.

Your pal,

Hulk Hagarson

362636 Starlet Drive
Hollywood, California

June 10

Dear V.,

Greetings from the Land of Sarandipity!

No, I haven't forgotten how to spell. *Sarandipity* is what I mean. Saran Wrap isn't just plastic; it's plastic you can see right through as though it weren't there.

Remember how in the old plays when you wanted to show a character who was insulated from the realities of life you would have that character wear white gloves? Today we insulate reality in Saran Wrap — Sarandipity!

From that soft and pliable Saran Wrap on the grocery-store food package, to that you-can't-get-me-open-with-a-blow-torch goo they laminate on all the other gadgets, instead of pigs in pokes today we buy pretty pictures in transparent packages — no odor, no texture, no touchee, no tastee.

Television presents its own parody-sical pictures the same way, and we see the world, not through a glass darkly, but through transparent plastic sparkly.

And we wonder that there are those who feel out of touch with reality, with life, with their own feelings, with themselves!

Real living requires real contact with real life! That's what I think Jesus is about, and that's what I think the church should be about.

So let me sign off:

Yours in the name of the
Master of Real Life!

Gloria Glitz

One Grecian Way
Toledo, Ohio

June 14

Dear Rev. Vertigo,

I took your advice and went to see a psychiatrist, but I don't think it's going to work.

He told me my problem stemmed from the fact that I love my mother and want to kill my father.

The fact of the matter is, however, that I was put out for adoption on the very same day that I was born, so I never even knew my father and mother. So how could I want to kill the one and have the other?

In the second place, when I was a young man and heard about this love-your-mother-kill-your-father thing, it horrified me. I knew I could never forgive myself for even thinking about a thing like that. So, just to be safe, I ran away from my adoptive home. No chance of incest or patricide, right?

So you see why I don't think much more of this psychiatrist thing than I do of your Christianity thing which tells me that God is my heavenly Father who loves me and forgives me.

I guess all I believe in is just fate.

Resignedly,

Eddie Poos

P.S. But there's a bright spot: I have just met this really attractive older woman, and I think it's Kismet.

ARMIN LEGG, M.D.
1998 Humerus Highway
Toledo, Ohio

June 18

Dear Mr. Versteeg,

I'm surprised at you — who as a pastor have to help so many people to deal with really serious illnesses — to become so upset over such a minor injury when it happens to you!

We almost never consider a case of tennis elbow terminal.

Do just as I told you: take two aspirin, rest your arm for a couple of weeks, and call me if it's not better.

You've only strained the tendon. Now, had you torn it loose, then you would have something to worry about, because a muscle pulled loose from the bone is about as useless and as harmful to the human body as is a Christian who is separated from the body of Christ.

The muscle itself may be good and big and healthy, but if it isn't attached and coordinated, it won't contribute anything useful to the work of the body. It'll only generate pain.

It's the same way as with a Christian who separates himself from the body of Christ, the church.

Maybe St. Paul learned that from Dr. Luke.

That reminds me. Please note your bill is enclosed. Blue Shield does not cover tennis elbow.

Sincerely,

Armin Legg, M.D.

MANNY'S GYM
Four Seasons Drive
Toledo, Ohio

June 22

Hey, Rev,

That quack who toll you to rest your tennis elbow, he's a quack.

What's more, he don't know nothin about sports medicine.

Here's what you do.

Warm up the arm real good. Then keep on liftin weights just like you always do except if it hurts too much. What you need is more strength in the arm.

Go ahead an play tennis. Just make sure you hit the backhands from the shoulder an lay off the topspin on the forehands.

In six months to a year, the pain will go away.

It's like a lotta things: a little pain don't necessarily mean you should quit. If you quit, it'll get worse.

Sometimes when you hurt, what you need ain't rest, but more an better work.

Tell your quack he should oughta quit livin in the Dark Ages an learn the modren way to treat tennis elbow.

An while you're at it, tell 'im the right name for it is *lateral epicondylitis.* One thing I can't stan is a illiterate quack.

Your pal,

Hulk Hagarson

ARMIN LEGG, M.D.
1998 Humerus Highway
Toledo, Ohio

June 27

To: All Area Clergy

Reverend Sir:

I write to alert you to an insidious challenge to Our Way of
Life.

I refer, of course, to the attempt of some so-called American
athletes to persuade us to allow a *chiropractor* to attend the
U.S. Olympic team.

That's right: a *chiropractor!*

These so-called American athletes — such as Dwight Stones,
Wilt Chamberlain, Alex Karras, and others — maintain that this
chiropractor has helped them — healing injuries, strengthening
muscles, improving performances — and would be able to help
our current Olympic athletes as well.

Obviously, theirs is a superstition. The chiropractor has
them psyched out.

We, however, who have earned our places in the medical
profession, are not going to sit back and allow this quack to
move in on our territory. As Chairman of the U.S. Olympic
Sports Medicine Committee of the American Medical Association, I promise you that we will resist to the last cot this attempt to include a chiropractor.

We M.D.s are the ones with the degrees; we are the ones
with the credentials; and we are the ones who know better than
the athletes themselves what is good for them.

I ask for your support in this effort, Pastor, because you
must surely see the close connection with your own professional
interests. You are a seminary graduate with a Master of Divinity
degree, perhaps even a Doctor of Ministry degree; you are a
properly ordained clergyman.

Therefore, you are the one who knows how to heal the souls
of your people. Now what would happen if some quack claimed

to have the Holy Spirit and actually healed your peoples' souls? I mean, what would your degrees signify then?

This affects all Christians. Card-carrying church members should be on guard against those who simply live by the Spirit of Christ and get results.

More deeply threatening to Our Way of Life is the threat this chiropractor poses to the very principles of Technicism. We have experts in our society. Experts know best. Experts not only know "how to," but "what to." Persons without proper credentials are sheep who need shepherding by experts.

I trust, Pastor, that you will recognize our common cause and that you will today write to the U.S. Olympic Committee supporting our rejection of the chiropractor.

Sincerely yours,

Armin Legg, M.D.

666 Shoehorn Manor
Toledo, Ohio

2 July

Versteeg:

No, I won't attend the committee meeting you called, and I don't especially appreciate your cluttering up my mail box with postcards about it, either.

Summer time is vacation time. I am entertaining friends on the weekends. I have to rest up from that. And when I'm rested, I have to start getting ready for the next weekend, so you see I don't have any spare time for those committee meetings you're so enamoured of.

Why don't you close up the church for the summer? We could give those missionaries long vacations, too. And there aren't many people in our hospitals and homes during the summer, are there?

What's so pressing about finances in the summer? With no heating bills, why does the church need money in hot weather?

Besides that, it must be a lot easier for you to work up sermons for the smaller number of people in church on a summer Sunday, so why don't we cut back on your inflated salary, too?

Contact me after Labor Day.

Forthrightly,

Henrietta Peckingham

53 Via Stromboli
Genoa, Ohio

July 7

Dear Roberto,

I was interested in that news item about that preacher who does sermons in ventriloquism.

I've been musing about whose voice it is we ought to hear when the preacher (you thought I was going to say *dummy*, didn't you?) opens his mouth.

Some want to hear echoing out of the preacher's mouth their own preferences and prejudices — St. Paul knew them as the people who have "itching ears." Their feline fixation is for just a little soothing scratching there.

Then there are those who, when the preacher opens his mouth, want to hear the voices of the contemporary scene. Their *"Newsweek* narcosis" listens only to reverberations in the public ear.

I'm not sure any of us could stand to hear the voice of God, were it not that the voice which pronounces judgment is the same voice which forgives.

Anyway, not many of us believe what we hear; most of us hear what we believe.

Ever think about just keeping your mouth shut?

Woodenly,

Pinoch

MANNY'S GYM
Four Seasons Drive
Toledo, Ohio

July 12

Hey, Rev,

   I was glad to see you liftin weights at Manny's the other night.

   You was doin OK, too — I mean considerin how old you are an everything.

   An I was thinkin it might do your soul some good, too, if three times a week you give your soul somethin a little heavier to lift.

   Like for example maybe you might try liftin up a little forgiveness for them foreign powers what been buggin us.

   Or pressin up some hope for the Washington regeem.

   Or pumpin up some enthusiasm for everyday things.

   You know what Joolius Caesar said about a sound soul in a sound body.

Your pal,

Hulk Hagarson

362636 Starlet Drive
Hollywood, California

July 16

Dear V.,

After one of those frantic weeks, last Sunday I went hiking in the hills around Hollywood with a friend who enjoys hiking as much as I do.

We discovered a tremendous ant hill. We stood and watched the activity seethe. Then my friend laughed and said, "I'll bet that's the way we must look to God — rushing around our petty ways while he gazes down in serenity."

After we started walking again — there in those hills that look so much like the hills in Palestine — I tried to explain that, no, I don't think God, remote and detached, looks at us like ants on an ant hill; that, far from it, I believe God sent his Spirit to inspire Moses and the prophets who spoke and acted in the crush of high-pressured daily life; that he took on the flesh of Jesus of Nazareth; that he entered completely into all our mass of human activity and brought his love there; and that God still walks with us moment by moment right here where we are, hiking with us even in our most frantic weeks.

I was thankful the Lord gave me that chance to witness above the ant hill.

Luv a Bunch!

Gloria Glitz

MANNY'S GYM
Four Seasons Drive
Toledo, Ohio

July 21

Hey, Rev,

I been thinkin' about how the Christian runs his course.

Way I see it, it's like bein on first base because you was a hit batsman, an then up to bat comes the Savior.

He parks one in the left-field bleachers.

An then the Christian is roundin third an headin for home.

All them RBIs belong to the Lord.

Your pal,

Hulk Hagarson

Heart of the Forest
Black Mountain
North Carolina

July 26

Dear Bob,

Here in the dog days I've been thinking how much the people of biblical times missed out on because they lived in a civilization that did not value dogs.

Back then, I know, dogs fell into the same ecological category with jackals and hyenas.

But I'm more in agreement with the Medieval church which made *canis,* the dog, a symbol for God, especially for God's faithfulness.

I know how John Masefield felt when he wrote:

Old Crafty wagged his tail
The day I first came home from jail.

Your dog knows no condemnation and carries no grudges. Your dog is always glad to see you.

So my dog teaches me what God's steadfast love is like. The way I read my Bible, God has a dogged love. No matter what, God is always glad to see us coming home.

Some philosopher said, "My dog recognizes me; therefore, I am." The ultimate is, "God loves me; therefore, I shall be."

The Fallen Angel is pictured with a tail. Do the other angels also have tails? Or, when a sinner repents or a Prodigal comes home, do they just wag their wings?

Truly yours,

Jonathan

Limestone Collegiate Church
Fort Industry Square
Toledo, Ohio

August 1

Dear Brother Versteeg,

Sorry, I won't be coming to the meeting.

It's too difficult to get to your church with the roads all torn up that way. It'll be nice when it's finished, though.

And while we're on the subject, this is a good time to take a look back down the road to see how you are doing with all those half-a-year-old New Year's resolutions you made last January 1.

Broad and easy is the road to destruction, Brother Versteeg, and paved with good intentions. The paths of righteousness are rocky roads of honor. Straight and narrow is the way that leads to life.

If you're still paving your roads only with good intentions, then you're bound to be traveling in the wrong direction.

I hope you're on track.

Just a word of brotherly advice.

Fraternally,

I. Rant

Dictated by Dr. Rant, but signed in his absence.

your Pal,
Hulk Hagarson

MANNY'S GYM
Four Seasons Drive
Toledo, Ohio

August 5

Hey, Rev,

I seen you strugglin with your lawnmower what has lost its power.

No use, Rev.

It's like a church what has lost its power — no matter how hard you push, it ain't gonna cut it.

Same way with folks. It ain't outside pushin they need, it's inside power.

Maybe Wolfgang can overhaul your mower insteada your car. Maybe that's somethin he can get to run.

As for power in the church an power in the people, for that kinda overhaulin you gotta take em to the Holy Spirit.

You don't need the push or the pull when you got the Power.

Your pal,

Hulk Hagarson

UNITED STATES POSTAL SERVICE
Rate at Increase
Toledo, Ohio
43611-537983-5729574-6749376-536489

August 9

Reverend Sir:

I am in receipt of complaints from several of your parishioners (their letters are available for your inspection during normal
business hours) who suspect that you have been fabricating and
mailing spurious letters.

I have subsequently been in touch with our Legal Depart-
ment who are reluctant to initiate formal action because of the
principle of separation of church and state, and because a
minor research assistant who has been thirty-eight years with
them reports that he has found some precedent for religious
people writing — well, fake letters — in what he terms the
"Pseudepigrapha." (When he identified these "pseudepigrapha"
as certain books of the Bible, our position became further ob-
scured legally because, although those original
"pseudepigrapha" were not circulated through the United States
mail, copies of the Bible now containing them are.)

Nevertheless, it appears to us that you are appealing to an
unadmirable, if common, desire on the part of persons to read
other persons' mail — a cavalier attitude which we cannot con-
done. What if St. Paul had done that?

I understand what you are trying to do, Rev. Versteeg; I
even sympathize, but I cannot approve. Whereas other
ministers' church-letter columns are proper and straight-forward
homilies, your game is to make up what you hope is an entertaining letter and along the way sneak in a religious point — as
if Christianity could be fun, or as if the Gospel needs to be
sugar-coated. Do you really think that is necessary? And I find
signing the letters with such transparent pseudonyms as "The
Rev. I. Rant" quite sophomoric.

I have nothing against religion. I am an active layman

myself. In fact, it's my personal belief that every Christian is, as St. Paul wrote to the Corinthians, a kind of two-legged letter, carrying by his or her life and testimony a message from the Sender.

Some of them, too, I'm afraid, are fake — not genuinely speaking the message of the Author whose signature they bear. And there are others, I'm sure I don't need to point out, who fail to address themselves to any purpose and thereby become undeliverable dead letters.

But as for your spurious letters, Rev. Versteeg, we do have to deal with the serious objection that some of your readers might become confused and might imagine that some of the letters in your "Letters to the Pastor" column of your church newsletter are, in fact, actual letters. You would not want that to happen, would you?

Therefore, just as I'm sure you would not want me to circulate spurious Christians, so I ask you, Rev. Versteeg, not as a matter of law, but as a matter of common courtesy, please to cease and desist from circulating spurious letters.

Sincerely Yours,

W. E. Luzit
Mail Fraud Inspector

ARMIN LEGG, M.D.
1998 Humerus Highway
Toledo, Ohio

August 12

Dear Mr. Versteeg,

Each of us has more than one of us inside his or her skin, more than one part to his or her personality.

Most of the time we can handle all the parts under one name — "I" or "me" — but at other times the different parts of our personalities become so sharply individuated and conflicted that we experience turmoil like, if not as intensely as, the Gadarene demoniac who told Jesus that his name was "Legion . . . because we are many."

I need to tell you that you have upset any number of people by publishing these "Letters to the Pastor" over the signatures of so many figments of your imagination and fragments of your personality.

There are people who think that Henrietta Peckingham is a real — more than real — member of your parish instead of a mere literary projection of your own paranoia. There are people who don't understand that Hulk Hagarson, Attila D. Hunn, Jonathan Woodman, Gloria Glitz, and all the rest are nothing more than several symptoms of your own schizophrenia.

People take you too seriously because you do not take yourself seriously enough.

Every personality needs to come together, Mr. Versteeg, no matter how many parts it has, and needs to unite in one personal identity. That is called wholeness.

One important function of Christianity can be to unite the personality — in Christianity, the person becomes one in Christ. The prescription to achieve that wholeness is constant prayer.

I diagnose your problem as too much city living. Why don't you move to some quiet little town?

Sincerely,

Armin Legg, M.D.

P.S. May we please have something on your account?

West Ohio Conference
471 E. Broad St. Suite P
Columbus, Ohio

August 16

My Dear Brother Versteeg,

You ask me why we United Methodists move our pastors around so often.

As if it were a fate reserved only for pastors! One-fifth of the population moves each year.

At least you are fortunate enough to be moving from a city to a small town instead of, as many must do, moving to bigger cities: you remember Archie Bunker's opinion of big cities like "Sodom and Glocca Morra"!

As for why we move our pastors, why don't you just consider it a parabolic reminder that we all of us are pilgrims and sojourners, dwellers in tents, and that no earthly home, no matter how clever the carpentry or massive the masonry — nothing made by human hands is our permanent home.

Jesus was trained as a carpenter and St. Paul as a tentmaker, but both were itinerant. They knew their real home to be with God, not made by hands, eternal in the heavens.

Thus, your moving may serve as an emblem to your people that we all of us have to move on in this world and eventually out of it to a new home.

Meanwhile, my advice to you is: Get a move on!

Episcopally,

Bishop Bright Roader

666 Shoehorn Manor
Toledo, Ohio

August 20

Lame Duck:

Don't think for a minute I'm not wise to you.

I knew you wouldn't last long in this church, but you're pulling out now just to try to get me to come back to church.

You think I've been using you as my excuse for copping out and not coming to church and not giving to the church.

Well, you're wrong. And if you think I'm going to let you trick me this way, you've got another think coming.

I'm not going to come back, and I'm not going to give one red cent — not until somebody down there does some real big shaping up.

At first I thought you were going to go where I told you to go, but they don't have churches there, do they?

Forthrightly,

Henrietta Peckingham

P.S. If at times I have had to be a little critical, it was only for your own good.

5630 Edgewater Drive
Toledo, Ohio

August 24

Dear Pastor Bob,

Maybe it's wrong for me to say this, but maybe Henrietta Peckingham was right.

At least she's not hurt.

Henrietta didn't get involved. She never tried to understand your style of ministry. She never tried to become a partner in it with you. So it doesn't hurt her now that you're leaving.

Don't you understand that those of us who did try to share ministry with you — well, now that you're leaving, we feel deserted and angry.

What are we supposed to do now — be partners with the next minister and then feel abandoned again when he leaves?

It's not easy, darn you!

How come every time you love you get hurt?

What are we supposed to do — just keep loving and keep getting hurt? I'm not God.

Thanks for the use of the hall.

Karen Cher

OK — love anyway. And luck!

666 Shoehorn Manor
Toledo, Ohio

28 August

Versteeg:

I hope you know how deeply you hurt me with that "P.S." in your letter to the members about your leaving.

Sure, we've had our differences of opinion, but I haven't been one of those two-faced people who only talk about your idiocy behind your back. When you've been wrong, I've always been willing to tell you so directly.

And when my wisdom and understanding have been rejected, I've stuck by you, knowing that a day would come when you'd need my advice again. Some thanks I get for my faithfulness!

In spite of it all, I'm too big-hearted to wish you ill, even after you made that nasty crack.

I hope there will be someone in your new church who will be willing to be as good a friend to you as I have been.

God bless you, and may you learn some day to recognize and appreciate your true friends!

With all my love,

Henrietta

P.S. I'm going to do all I can to help our new pastor when he arrives. I have high hopes. Isn't there some rule that the Bishop isn't allowed to send us two losers in a row?

(Note: Henrietta's letter was forwarded to me by the Rev. Howard Abts.)

—Portrait by
Henrietta

Robert John Versteeg

Robert Versteeg has been a preacher, a teacher, a writer, a director and actor (he hoped that would qualify him to be either President or Pope, whichever offer came first) — and it all started from his humble beginnings as custodian in a bookstore. He probably should still be in custody.

Versteeg is the father of three children who by comparison are only a little strange.

— Henrietta Peckingham